# THE LONG, LONG WAR

# THE LONG LONG WAR

## COUNTERINSURGENCY IN MALAYA AND VIETNAM

Brigadier Richard L. Clutterbuck

FOREWORD BY

GENERAL HAROLD K. JOHNSON
*Chief of Staff, United States Army*

FREDERICK A. PRAEGER, *Publishers*

New York • Washington

BOOKS THAT MATTER

Published in the United States of America in 1966
by Frederick A. Praeger, Inc., Publishers
111 Fourth Avenue, New York 3, N. Y.

Library of Congress Catalog Card Number: 66-13678

Printed in the United States of America

TO

BOB NULSEN *and* BOB OSBORN

*two of those who fought through*

*the dark years in Vietnam, 1962–65*

# FOREWORD

**D**EEP within each human breast is a yearning for something better for himself and for his family, regardless of his station or position in life. This yearning is translated into ceaseless search for a better life for all mankind. Modern communications, visual and audible, coupled with modern transportation have accelerated the tempo of the search. The story is told of a young man in a newly independent country walking the streets of his capital city for the first time, with hand extended, asking for his share of "freedom." He knew the word. He understood the word held high promise, but he did not know what it meant, nor did he know of the responsibilities that freedom imposed upon himself or upon his countrymen. The creation of an independent democratic government is a most difficult process. For the leadership, it means avoiding that ancient danger expressed in the axiom: "Power tends to corrupt; absolute power corrupts absolutely." For the individual, it means acceptance of the full responsibility of sustaining his government.

The object of lawful government is the establishment of a stable society which can grow and prosper in an atmosphere of justice and order.

Wars are fought to impose control or to resist the imposition of control.

Over the years, both the United States and Great Britain have supported the objective of lawful government and have resisted the imposition of control by outsiders, not only over their own lands but also over those of other nations with like beliefs. Neither has sought in modern times to impose its own control over others.

Those nations and peoples which cherish freedom and justice under a lawful government of their own choosing are now challenged by a new strategy—with a new body of supporting tactics—which we call "insurgency" and others call "wars of national liberation." Those that foment insurgency are content to wait years before gaining their aims and are, therefore, often found representing themselves as anything but what they really are, and saying anything but what they really believe. They know full well the value of patience to ensure that their efforts are timely and unified. Frequently, this type of conflict has been supported by outsiders whose aim is not to provide those cherished desires but to ensure that they are not a part of the government ultimately to be established.

The weapons used in insurgency are initially simple by modern standards. The tactics are frequently both abhorrent and seemingly senseless. It is a tremendous mistake, however, to assume that insurgent wars are simple wars because the weapons are simple. It is an even greater mistake to assume that the seemingly senseless tactics stem from leaders who are themselves senseless.

The insurgencies in Malaya and Vietnam are very sophisticated wars. Every conceivable facet of human life and endeavor and every function and agency of government have been taken under attack by every available means. Those wars are a blend of intense political, economic, socio-psychological, and military activities—a blend conceived, practiced, and finally put into operation by experts. The result is total war, war more total in its effect on people than any ever fought before.

Coping with insurgencies requires an equally well blended wide range of efficient and effective activities, equally well directed. But the problem is not so easily solved as this would indicate.

One of the key strategies of insurgency, or "wars of national liberation," is initially to create a disorder which can later be exploited, penetrating every institution to the maximum degree possible to promote confusion, disagreement, and uncertainty. The counterinsurgent's task is to maintain the established order while in fact waging war against the insurgents who are spread among the population. The counterinsurgent is thus constrained against the use of force which would normally be acceptable against a completely hostile population. The arms of the government must be long enough to reach out to all of the people, firm enough to give them support, and strong enough to protect them from coercion and outside influence.

Every person, soldier or civilian, must be an agent of all branches of government and prepared to back up or fill in where needed. In the District Teams in Vietnam, a combat arms captain is charged with advising his counterparts in military, psycho-social, economic, and political matters, and though the degree of expertise varies from man to man, it has been a most successful undertaking.

A second key insurgency strategy is that purely military victory neither necessarily wins nor loses the broader war. The insurgent purpose of the military aspect is to create the disorder for exploitation by economic, political, and socio-psychological means. Since both the insurgent and the counterinsurgent are likely to create disorder on the military side, regardless of how the latter tries to avoid it, the ultimate final victory rests with the political, economic, and socio-psychological outcomes.

A close integration of the political, economic, information, security, and military branches of government is essential to ensure a concentration of effort against an insurgency. One must constantly keep foremost in mind that military action is only a part of counterinsurgency and that a well-integrated "team" can often compound a military success or minimize a failure.

There are many similarities and some differences in the insurgent wars in Malaya and Vietnam, as the author points out. I believe that the major difference from the standpoint of the governments and peoples of Great Britain and the United States is that although Great Britain has for many years had an interest in Malaya, the United States' interest in Vietnam is relatively young. Thus the United States is starting from scratch in Vietnam whereas Great Britain started from a base of environmental experience in its aid and assistance to Malaya.

One must keep in mind that while the *modus operandi* of most insurgencies is the same, the actual applications may be quite dissimilar. The variable is not simply geographical configuration and climate but is, more importantly, the people, their degree of development, their existing form of government, their religion, and— most important—their attitude toward their government. Just as the insurgent considers each of the conditions just mentioned, exploiting those that best suit him, the counterinsurgent must improve those that are satisfactory while combating the insurgents' efforts where conditions are being exploited. This is rarely a combat operation, but is more often a battle for the hearts and minds of the people. When one side or the other can communicate with, and appeal to, the mass of the people, they are several steps farther on the road to victory. In Greece and Malaya, Cuba and Cyprus, many of the people had chosen their side before the shooting began, but those who were wooed to one side or the other during the conflict weighed heavily on the outcome.

Both the author of this book and the writer of this Foreword are professional soldiers. It may come as a surprise to the layman that the professional military of both Great Britain and the United States agree upon the broader aspects of this form of conflict. Over the years both countries have become fairly expert. Both are becoming more expert day by day.

The author of this book served as the United Kingdom Liaison Officer to the Command and General Staff College at Fort Leavenworth, Kansas, when this writer was the Commandant. The author prepared and presented several periods of instruction to more than 1,500 resident United States and Allied officer students each of the two years of his tour. His contributions to the evolving doctrine for countering insurgency were significant, and his presentations on the same subject were stimulating and provocative. As knowledge of his ability became more widespread, he was in demand as a guest lecturer at the service schools and colleges of all of the Services. He gave unstintingly of his talent and time. He has been and continues to be a true and respected friend of the United States Army.

HAROLD K. JOHNSON
*Washington, D.C.*                      General, United States Army
*February, 1966*                                    Chief of Staff

# ACKNOWLEDGMENTS

I HAVE bothered many of my friends and acquaintances—Malayan, American, and British—to fill in the gaps in my knowledge and to correct some of my mistakes. I would like particularly to acknowledge the help of:

Mr. J. L. H. Davis, C.B., D.S.O., who not only served right through the Communist insurgency but had previously served *with* the Communist guerrillas against the Japanese in World War II;

Brigadier D. L. Lloyd Owen, D.S.O., O.B.E., M.C., who was Military Assistant to General Sir Gerald Templer from 1952 to 1954;

Mr. Mohamad Shariff, A.M.N., P.I.S., P.K.S., a distinguished member of the Malayan Police Special Branch, who brought off one of the most successful coups of the insurgency and has since earned further laurels in the confrontation with Indonesia;

Major General A. G. Patterson, D.S.O., O.B.E., M.C., who

served with the Gurkhas through many years of the insurgency, commanded the Brigade that dealt with the Brunei revolt in 1962, and continued thereafter in Sarawak against the Indonesian incursions; Lieutenant Colonel Charles K. Nulsen, Jr., U.S. Army, who served in Vietnam (Zone D) in 1962–63 and found time to correspond with me both while I was instructing his fellow Americans in counterinsurgency and ever since;

Major Robert B. Osborn, U.S. Army, who also made time to keep up a most invigorating correspondence while he was fighting in Quang Ngai Province in 1964–65.

Among them they have commented on most of my first draft, and some have sat discussing it far into the night. They are not, however, in any way responsible for the final version or for the facts and opinions, and still less for the errors and misjudgments, which are mine alone.

RICHARD CLUTTERBUCK

*Singapore*
*March, 1966*

# CONTENTS

# MAPS AND CHARTS

# THE LONG, LONG WAR

# INTRODUCTION:

# MALAYA IN PERSPECTIVE—
# AND VIETNAM

The answer lies not in pouring more troops into the jungle, but in the hearts and minds of the people.

— GENERAL TEMPLER, *Malaya, 1952*

The Revolution was effected before the war commenced. The Revolution was in the minds and hearts of the people.

—JOHN ADAMS, *U.S.A., 1818*

. . . which goes to show that the British have been learning the same lessons about counterinsurgency for nearly 200 years.

I was born fourteen days after the Communist Revolution in Russia, so in 1945 we both became twenty-eight years old. In every year since then, British soldiers have had to fire in anger against some kind of revolutionary activity directed or exploited by Communism. If Russian Communism seems to have mellowed, as befits a man nearing fifty, its wildcat child in China has not, and the shooting goes on.

This kind of war has clearly come to stay, and its manifestations will extend from a quick, bloodless takeover, as in Czechoslovakia in 1948, to a long and violent conflict, as in Malaya and Vietnam, sometimes escalating to a Korea or a Dien Bien Phu. The insurgency in Malaya covered quite a large part of this spectrum and threatened to cover it all; it was ended by a victory that, though

3

gradual and unspectacular, was as complete and enduring as any such victory is ever likely to be.

Counterinsurgency has been headline news for so long that such phrases as "winning the hearts and minds" and "separating the guerrillas from the people" have become platitudes. The problem is how to accomplish these ends.

In this book, I describe how we accomplished them in Malaya from 1948 to 1960. I served there from 1956 to 1958, and during this period Malaya became independent. Like many other British soldiers and civilians, I stayed on after Independence Day as an employee of the new Malayan Government. Those were great days to be in Malaya, to see a new nation getting under way and a full-scale Communist insurgency crumbling in its path.

The story is in three parts: the *defensive,* in which we prevented the enemy from taking over and kept the insurgency from escalating; the *offensive,* in which the enemy's power to beat us was broken; and the *victory,* in which the Communists were hunted down and destroyed, and an independent Malaya was established on a stable and prosperous path—the end product.

The theme of the defensive phase was *security,* and it had a civil and a military side. The civil problem was to retain the thread of government control in each village through an unintimidated police post and a local administration with the strength and will to enforce decisions of the central government. Otherwise, the central government could have done no more than "legislate in a void," as the French described it in Vietnam. The military problem was to relieve the pressure on the villages by forcing the big guerrilla units to split up. This would not have been achieved if we had stuck to our original overambitious plans to destroy them outright. Breaking them up into units of manageable size requires very different tactics.

The theme of the offensive was *intelligence*—not high-level military intelligence on maps, but basic police intelligence at the Communists' own grass roots. This became more important than military tactics, about which (once the guerrillas had been prevented from escalating into conventional forces) there was no particular mystery. When our soldiers made contact with the guerrillas, the soldiers nearly always won because their chance to train had been so much greater. In Malaya we killed or captured six guerrillas for every soldier or policeman they got. The problem was putting the forces into contact, and this depended on getting information from the people on whom the guerrillas relied for support.

There is a popular fallacy that this kind of information will flow into our hands if we simply "get the majority of the people on our side." Certainly we must get majority support eventually if the victory is to last, but it plays little part in how we actually win. Caught between armed guerrillas and armed policemen or soldiers, the bulk of the people will be on neither side. They will just hope that one or the other wins soon and gets it all over. Only a few dedicated Communists or close relatives will voluntarily risk their necks for guerrillas. With the rest, the guerrillas must be tough enough to ensure their general acquiescence (otherwise there would be no insurgency); but they will need to coerce only about 10 per cent of them to give active support.

We devised a technique for persuading a handful of the active but unwilling supporters to become our agents and betray the Communists. This, coupled with our exploitation of surrendered guerrillas, was how we defeated them; and the mass of the people accepted the end of their ordeal with relief.

In the third phase, the theme was *government:* at the top, a stable central government, subject to popular control, supported by a broad base of civil servants, professional men, and technicians, to administer the people and make the economy grow; at the grass roots, effective local government, backed by a police force that enabled it to function without coercion or corruption. During the final stages of the insurgency, while the roots of Communism were being dug out, the establishment of civil administration took priority over everything. The Malaya that evolved has grown in strength and stature despite an explosive racial mixture and a hostile confrontation by a pro-Communist neighbor ten times its size.

The insurgency in Malaya must be put into perspective with the two original models of Communist revolutions, in Russia and in China, and with its two sister insurgencies in North and South Vietnam. Although no two insurgencies are quite the same, certain common factors emerge that are as constant as the principles of war.

The Russian and Chinese patterns of revolution are quite separate—one owing its origin to Lenin and the other to Mao Tse-tung. Most revolutionary leaders begin by trying the Russian pattern; it is quicker. If they are balked, as in North Vietnam and Malaya, they revert to Mao Tse-tung's "protracted war." Both methods are effective, have the same aim, and are directed by a small elite Party; but they are very different in execution.

The Russian pattern is urban, culminating in a *coup d'état* in which the central control of the country (or part of it) is seized by a combination of political maneuvering, organized rioting, and capture of key points. Control of the army and the police (from above or from within) is a major factor, but there is little attempt to win widespread public support until power has been seized.

The Chinese pattern is rural. A far longer and more exhausting process, it develops only when the Russian pattern will not work— for example, when the country is such that control of the cities does not give control of the rural areas (as in China) or when the people in the cities are not ripe for Communist control (as in Malaya and Vietnam). The revolutionaries must therefore turn to guerrilla warfare, which relies utterly on the support of the people.

Chinese leadership, not Russian, constitutes the danger in the developing countries of the world. The Russian Communists have little understanding of guerrilla warfare or of organizing popular support for guerrillas; even in their own country under German occupation they were surprisingly unsuccessful.

Mao Tse-tung grounded his theories on the need for getting support from the simple people. Ho Chi Minh in Vietnam and Chin Peng in Malaya did likewise. They were willing to work for years to win popular support, and this makes their revolutionary technique much more dangerous; it also provides us with a clear indication of the way—the only way—such revolutions can be defeated.

Ho Chi Minh, after an unsuccessful attempt at a *coup d'état* on the Russian model in 1946, faithfully followed the Mao Tse-tung plan in North Vietnam. Harnessing the anticolonial movement for national independence to Communist aims and organization, he built up a cell system in the villages to provide support for the guerrillas in the form of intelligence, counterintelligence, food, money, and sabotage of government forces and installations. Although local and decentralized, these village organizations were subject to the usual underground system of control from the top through committees at province and district level. They were ready to emerge into the open as a going concern when French control was ousted. This clandestine system of government is known as the parallel hierarchy.

The Communists also raised village terror squads, armed with captured weapons, whose task was to make examples of "traitors" and above all to eliminate or intimidate local government officials, so that real control of the people would fall into the hands of the parallel hierarchy.

Alongside the political organization, and subject to its control, Vo Nguyên Giap built up the Vietminh military organization. This too began at the bottom. Village squads of ten or fifteen men were formed, holding secret caches of weapons. Squads formed platoons, and platoons were affiliated to companies based on the local market town. These in turn formed district battalions, which were the highest units of the part-time militia or people's armed forces. The best soldiers and units graduated to regional forces, and finally to the regular army. Their task became much easier in 1949, when Mao Tse-tung's army reached the southern frontiers of China, giving Giap's regular forces an "active sanctuary"[1] in which to organize, train, and gather heavier equipment. By 1950, they were ready to force the French to abandon their frontier posts. In 1951–52, they tried to escalate the war from the guerrilla to the conventional stage by concentrating in big units to attack fixed French positions. The attempt was premature, and they suffered heavily. They reverted to guerrilla warfare and soon made French control of the villages illusory, except in the Red River Delta around Hanoi. Then, with wide popular support, ample sources of recruits, and safe areas in which to train them, Giap again built up his regular army. The French tactics played into his hands, and he was able to gather the strength to attack and defeat them in a set-piece battle at Dien Bien Phu in 1954. The war in the North was over. Apart from the premature attempt at escalation in 1951–52, it was a model performance.

After the 1954 Geneva Conference on Indochina, large numbers of Vietnamese moved from South to North, and vice versa. Some

---

[1] Bernard B. Fall, *Street Without Joy: Insurgency in Indochina 1946–1963*, p. 357. (When not given in the footnote, publication information can be found in the Bibliography.)

90,000 South Vietnamese went to the North. Mainly these were men serving in Vietminh units, and from them Ho Chi Minh trained the guerrilla cadres who were to return South to form the core of the Viet Cong a few years later. At the same time, he built up his underground organization and the village squads for his people's army, using agents already in South Vietnam and others sent in among the million refugees from the North. He was convinced that internal strife between rival religious sects would soon cause the South Vietnamese government to collapse, leaving his parallel hierarchy in control.

To President Ngo Dinh Diem's credit, however, his young government did not collapse. It quelled the internal dissension; and South Vietnam, with aid from the United States, became far more prosperous than the North. Refugees from that area told of food shortages, and collectivization of land held no appeal for South Vietnamese farmers, who were mostly tilling their own land. Communism was clearly losing ground.

In 1957, therefore, Ho Chi Minh decided that positive steps were necessary to break the Diem regime. He launched the underground Viet Cong terror squads on a campaign of murder and intimidation to destroy the fabric of local government, just as he had done in North Vietnam ten years earlier. It was only after the launching of this campaign that Diem's government began to lose popularity. He answered the Communist terror by imposing restrictions, but he failed to establish a local government and police force strong enough either to enforce the restrictions or to protect citizens from Communist retribution. The villagers thus had little option but to obey the Viet Cong.

Meanwhile, the Viet Cong built up their regional and regular forces as the Vietminh had done. The South Vietnamese Army, trained and equipped to meet a Korean-type conventional invasion, proved just as unsuited for dealing with a guerrilla enemy[2] as the French. The Viet Cong were able to operate in units of ever-increasing size, making protection of the villages more and more difficult.

President Diem lost the confidence of his people in a vicious

---

[2] Bernard B. Fall, *The Two Viet-Nams: A Political and Military Analysis*, p. 325.

spiral. They resented being punished for giving in to a coercion from which they had no protection. A vast resettlement program tore many of them away from their land, bringing hardship without the compensation of real security. By 1963, the government was so unpopular that it was only a matter of time before it had to go. Its violent end was followed by eight changes of government in little more than a year.

In 1964, Ho Chi Minh judged that the time was near for escalation into conventional war. He stepped up his infiltration of reinforcements across the border. Since the pool of Southerners who had come North in 1954 had largely dried up, many of these reinforcements were of North Vietnamese stock. The Viet Cong began to operate in larger units and became more aggressive. The South Vietnamese and United States governments decided to answer this escalation by direct retaliation against its source in North Vietnam.

Although counterinsurgency in South Vietnam was still in the defensive stage, there had already been three critical periods in the war.

The first was in 1957–58, when terrorist murders of civilians were on the same scale as in Malaya in 1948. In Malaya, they were recognized for what they were, and drastic action was taken. In South Vietnam, the government, even as late as 1959, was strangely complacent; the parallel hierarchy had effective clandestine control over much of the population before any serious shooting began.

The second was in 1962–63, when government action failed either to establish control and protection of the population or to prevent the Viet Cong from operating in units of ever-growing size. Malaya faced a similar crisis in 1950–51, but it was weathered successfully and set the stage for the offensive phase.

Despite many differences and great difficulties, the means were available for a favorable resolution of these crises in South Vietnam. If they had been resolved, the third crisis would never have arisen in 1965, in which the undercurrent of subversion and terror continued, but the main war escalated. This crisis had no equivalent in Malaya because the earlier battles had gone the right way.

Whatever other crises there may be, the final problem in Vietnam lies ahead—to dig out the roots of subversion and guerrilla Communism. After we had spent six years breaking the Communists' aggressive power in Malaya, it took six more years to dig out these roots. Some of the lessons we learned will be of value when that time comes in Vietnam.

Nor will Vietnam be the last area where the U.S. or Britain will help to counter Communist insurgency. Wherever the other outbreaks may occur—in Asia, Africa, or Latin America—and whether by subversion, *coup d'état,* rioting, or guerrilla warfare, we must not repeat the mistakes made in Malaya (from which, luckily, we learned in time) and in Vietnam. That is the reason for this book.

ONE

# DEFENSIVE (1945-51)

# 1

# GROWTH OF A
# COMMUNIST PARTY

L IKE most other Communist movements, the Malayan Communist Party (MCP) had an urban beginning. From the start, it competed with the Kuomintang in trying to gain control of the overseas Chinese, who made up 38 per cent of the population of Malaya—by far the highest overseas Chinese proportion in any nation.

Agents from China, starting work in Hong Kong and Singapore in 1924, found little support. Most of the Chinese in these cities are intensely commercial, and such support as the Communists achieved was, and always remained, largely from two racial groups socially despised by other Chinese, the Hakkas and the Hailams. By 1928, however, the agents had established a South Seas Communist Party in Singapore and were able to organize an effective strike that year. In 1930, the Malayan Communist Party was formed. An important conference that year in Singapore was at-

13

tended by Ho Chi Minh, the leader of a Vietnamese movement in exile based in Hong Kong. These activities were directed not by Mao Tse-tung but by the Russian Communist Party's Far Eastern Bureau in Shanghai.

Western intelligence services were not unaware of these developments. In the Singapore Police Force, the Head of the Special Branch (the British term for police intelligence) was a Mr. Onraet. Onraet surmised that a high Communist Party official was certain to visit the South Seas group. His suspicions fell on a supposed French commercial traveler who had set up an office overlooking the harbor but seemed to do very little business. He called himself Serge Le Franc, but the Special Branch identified him as Joseph Ducroix, an important international Communist. Onraet hired an office near that of Ducroix, whose visitors were carefully watched. In time, Ducroix's office and the homes of other Communists revealed by the watch were raided simultaneously. The haul included numerous addresses in Singapore, Hong Kong, and Shanghai.

Among these addresses was that of Ho Chi Minh, who was arrested in Hong Kong and imprisoned until 1932. Much more important at that time, however, were the addresses in Shanghai, where the seizure of Communist archives resulted in the virtual disruption of the whole Far Eastern Bureau. It was two years before any coordinated Communist activity was resumed in Southeast Asia—a remarkable dividend for one piece of astute intelligence work.

Among those who escaped the net was Lai Tek, a young Vietnamese who had met Ho Chi Minh in Hong Kong. This was the first of Lai Tek's remarkable escapes from capture by both the British and the Japanese. These escapes have given rise to the theory that he was enlisted by the British Special Branch in Hong Kong and installed as a British agent in the Malayan Communist Party, so remaining until his disappearance in 1947. There is an intriguing possibility that Lai Tek may have been a triple agent. He was certainly a member of the Communist Party, and there is strong evidence that he worked not only with the British but with the Japanese. Perhaps all three sides were under the impression that he was "their" man. Whether he was in fact a British agent or posed as an agent may never be officially confirmed or denied. But if he was in touch with the Special Branch, the police officers who handled him will never be completely sure where his true loyalty lay.

Lai Tek arrived in Singapore in 1934 with an impressive tale that he had been trained in Russia and France. He supported this with a convincing knowledge of Marxist theory and brilliant organizing ability. There is now little doubt that he had never been in Russia or France, but his knowledge and ability were genuine enough. By 1939, he had organized a cell system on the authentic model all over Malaya, and that year he was unanimously elected Secretary General of the Malayan Communist Party.

His achievements as Secretary General meant much trouble for the British, but do not by any means rule out the possibility that he was a British agent. The standard practice for agents is to work for their "target" organization to the full extent of their talent, on the grounds that if they were not holding the post it would be held by someone else as good or better, who would not be an agent. The true agent—be he a Communist plant in our ranks or a Western plant with the Communists—can best be looked for among the most efficient members of his organization, and if he is the head of it so much the better.

The Malayan Communist Party's aim and function were reversed when Russia suddenly became an ally of the British in 1941. The Japanese invaded Malaya at the end of the year; and Lai Tek was instructed to offer all possible help to the British against the Japanese, including the organization of guerrilla warfare in the rear of the Japanese armies.

The meeting that followed between Lai Tek and the British must have presented an intriguing situation for both sides if in fact he was a British agent. It was conducted with all the proper aura of a conspiracy, behind dark glasses and locked doors. The British agreed to train and equip "stay-behind parties" of Communist guerrillas. In the four weeks remaining before Singapore fell, they trained 200. These men set up camps in the jungle; and during the next three years they created a Chinese guerrilla force, the Malayan People's Anti-Japanese Army (MPAJA), containing 7,000 men organized in eight regiments. More important than the regiments, however, was the powerful supporting organization built up in the Chinese villages and among the "squatters"—isolated Chinese homesteaders who had staked a claim without title on patches of land on the jungle fringes to grow food for themselves.

In characteristic Communist style, the guerrillas were in no hurry. Their first task was to create the organization, not to invite destruction by starting the shooting too soon. In the long run, they would thereby be better placed to destroy the Japanese control of the country. If, however, the Japanese were evicted by the British first, the ultimate aim would be the original one—to oust the British. Meanwhile, the guerrillas had no more qualms about cooperating with the British than Mao Tse-tung had about working with the Kuomintang. The Malayan Communists made sure that they took more from the British than they gave; and by the time the first atomic bomb had burst, the guerrillas had done little to embarrass the Japanese.

The Allies judged it best, in both Malaya and Europe, to cooperate with anyone who would help them win the war. They were content to face up to the postwar consequences when they arose. It is still too early to judge whether this policy was wise.

Certainly the British officers working with the guerrillas had no illusions about their eventual aim. British soldiers, including the man who in 1942 trained the cadre of 200, Colonel Spencer Chapman, stayed behind in the jungle with the guerrillas. The following year, the guerrillas were joined by Force 136, a unit similar to the U.S. Military Assistance Advisory Groups, which eventually reached a strength of 40 officers and about 250 noncommissioned officers and radio operators. Force 136 organized the delivery by submarine and parachute of arms, ammunition, equipment, and supplies, and acted as a link with the Allied Commander in Chief, Lord Louis Mountbatten, in preparing the guerrillas to act in support of the intended landings (which were in the event preceded by Hiroshima and the Japanese surrender). Force 136 was led by Colonel John Davis, who had helped organize the stay-behind parties and was personally known to some of the guerrillas. Davis became a friend and associate of Chin Peng, the Party Secretary in the state of Perak, who was destined to become Secretary General of the Malayan Communist Party in 1947. As well as being responsible for the underground "People's Organization" in this important state, Chin Peng was assigned by the Party as their liaison officer with the Allied High Command, through Davis and Force 136.

Davis had orders not to discuss politics and to cooperate with the Communists in defeating the Japanese without expressing any views on the future of Malaya after the war. The Communists cooperated well but left him in no doubt of the Party's eventual intention to establish a Communist republic. They probably genuinely hoped that the British would remain their allies on this basis.

Chin Peng himself almost certainly held this view. At the time, he was only twenty-two and had no idea that he would later be Secretary General of the Communist Party or that he would lead a full-scale Communist insurgency against the British.

Chin Peng emerges from this whole story as one of the more attractive Communist personalities. Few people who have worked with him, either in World War II or later in the abortive truce talks in 1955, deny that he is likable, intelligent, and sincere. John Davis has no doubt that Chin Peng, as a good Communist, would have cut his throat if the Party had so required, but that all the same he was an honest and agreeable colleague. It is a tragedy that his tremendous ability and leadership should have been channeled in a direction that hindered rather than helped the development of the thriving postwar Federation of Malaya.

In 1942, however, Chin Peng was only a State Secretary, and a fervent admirer of the man who was then Secretary General, Lai Tek.

Lai Tek did not live in the jungle, though he sometimes visited it and had two conferences with Davis and Chapman. He was based on Singapore Island, where he lived comfortably and drove a powerful car, in which he seems to have had no difficulty passing through the Japanese checkpoint on the only causeway across the Straits of Johore to the mainland. This, however, is not the only factor that gives rise to the theory that, as well as being a Communist and a British agent, he was working with the Japanese.

In August, 1942, the Central Committee of the Malayan Communist Party was raided in almost full session by the Japanese. In this raid and in subsequent arrests, the entire Committee was captured. But Lai Tek, "unavoidably" late for the meeting, escaped; and he was thus left as the sole important Communist official in Singapore, which suited him well.

A month later, a meeting of leading Communists from the jungle was summoned in the Batu caves, in central Malaya. These caves seemed to offer a secure meeting place. There was only one entrance, from which there were long fields of observation for the guerrillas posted to guard it. But the Japanese, aware of this meeting in advance, had troops in waiting, and ninety-one Communists were killed or captured. Once again, Lai Tek miraculously escaped.

The evidence, now accepted by the British and by the Malayan Communists, strongly suggests that both these meetings were betrayed by Lai Tek to the Japanese and that this betrayal was their price for allowing him to continue to operate as Secretary General. This is consistent with the rest of the Lai Tek story. The Japanese were content to let the Communist organization grow, provided it had "their" man at the head. Lai Tek, whether a true Communist or a triple agent, was content with the chance to establish his own power, with all his rivals and potential betrayers eliminated.

It can be argued that his staging of the destruction by the Japanese of virtually the entire top level of the Communist leadership in Malaya was a brilliant coup in his role as a British agent. This theory, I am sure, is untenable. The British were at that time going through their darkest period of the war, in Europe, North Africa, and the Far East. They were desperate for allies who could help them hold the Japanese and were doing their utmost to strengthen, train, and arm the Communist guerrillas. That they should at that moment sponsor the disruption of the Malayan Communist leadership does not make sense, particularly since those eliminated included all who were critical of Lai Tek's live-and-let-live policy toward the Japanese. If Lai Tek really was a British agent, the form and effect of his cooperation with the Japanese proves that he was certainly not solely a British agent.

Whatever his true motives, the Communists themselves at this time had no suspicion of him. He emerged from the war with an enhanced reputation as a brilliant organizer who led a charmed life, and the Party was at the peak of its power and prestige.

# 2

# RECIPE FOR CHAOS

IF the Chinese guerrillas and their Chinese supporters ended World War II on a high note, the other races in Malaya certainly did not.

Malaya in 1945 (excluding the Colony of Singapore) had a population of about 5 million, of whom 49 per cent were Malays, 38 per cent Chinese, and 12 per cent Indians. The remaining 1 per cent were Europeans, Eurasians, and seminomadic aborigine tribesmen (like Vietnam's *montagnards*) living in the mountainous jungle that covers four-fifths of Malaya.

It is important to distinguish between "Malayan" and "Malay." The Malays are a race, but all the races in Malaya are Malayans, just as the Scotsmen in Britain are British and Negroes in America are Americans. The Malays recognized the sovereignty of the Malay Sultans, who had ruled their states for more than a thousand years. The Chinese and Indians were immigrants and retained their racial identity.

The Malays, who are believed to have emigrated originally from the Melanesian islands of the Pacific, are very different in character from the industrious Chinese. It may well be due to the lush, relaxing climate of Malaya, where the temperature and humidity stay much the same through the year, and where, once a man has cleared a bit of jungle, he can grow abundant food for himself, his wives (up to four), and his children with so little work that the Malays have become one of the most easygoing, uncommercial, unambitious—and charming—races in the world. They have also, for many centuries, been Moslems; and their religion has further contributed to their lack of ambition for power or worldly goods and their acceptance of an undemanding paternal rule by their Sultans.

Up to the sixteenth century, the Malays had little contact with the outside world except for the Moslem traders from the Middle East, who converted them to Islam but did not settle in any numbers. Thereafter, however, seafaring traders from Portugal, Holland, France, and Britain anchored off the coasts and were generally welcomed. Both sides gained from the trading settlements on the offshore islands of Singapore and Penang, and in the coastal areas of Malacca; these three became British colonies early in the nineteenth century. Though they traded with the Malay states in the hinterland, the British had no thought of ruling those states. Later in the century, they responded to requests from the Sultans for British civil servants to help their administration, and subsequently for protection. But at no time, until the arrival of the Japanese, had the Malays been ruled by anyone other than their own Sultans, though in the latter decades the Sultans ruled by agreement with the British.

During the last half of the nineteenth century, British commercial enterprise and investment flourished in Malaya, notably with the development of the rich tin and rubber industries. Since the Malays preferred their easy agricultural life, they were content to see laborers coming in from China and India to do the work. These laborers had no citizenship rights, and their general intention was to return to China or India richer men—as many did. Many others, however, stayed. The Chinese soon bloomed into a thriving commercial society, with its millionaires, middlemen, and hard-working coolies. They brought enormous prosperity to the country and left the administration and policing to the British and Malays.

The Japanese occupation brought this structure crashing down. The British administrators, tin miners, and rubber planters were imprisoned, and the mines and plantations fell into chaos. Many Chinese, left without work, set up small holdings on abandoned land near the fringes of the jungle. The number of Chinese squatters swelled to 400,000—about half the Chinese rural population.

The Japanese did their utmost to play up racial feeling between the Malays and Chinese, hoping to win over the Malays by showing them preference and consideration. The Malays have been criticized for tolerating Japanese rule, but this was just as much in character as their acceptance of the British. The Chinese, however, regarded the Japanese as bitter enemies and the Malays as traitors. The Japanese encouraged the Malays to regard the Chinese—and particularly the Communists—as immigrant bandits disrupting the Malay homeland. Certainly most of the rural Chinese, whether guerrillas, villagers, or squatters, did their best to hamper the Japanese regime; and this further increased their hardships.

Then, in August, 1945, came the surrender of the Japanese Government to the Allies. The British reoccupation force that arrived three weeks later was greeted with enthusiasm by most of the people, who were glad to see the war over. They rallied to the re-establishment of British administration, which they remembered as just and orderly.

The Malayan Communist Party's Central Committee was now in something of a dilemma. The Party was not in a position to govern. Also, in the discussions among Davis, Chapman, Lai Tek, and Chin Peng in the jungle, the Communists had agreed to co-operate in re-establishing British rule when the Japanese were evicted. This was no doubt a promise to be discarded when convenient, as any other Communist means to an end, but in 1945 they dared not discard it yet. Ho Chi Minh was facing similar problems in Hanoi; he had to accept a brief period of cooperation with France. The Malayan Communists probably were glad to let the British lessen the chaos before they took over. The Central Committee foresaw little difficulty in doing this when the time came.

After some reluctance, the Communists agreed to disband the guerrilla army and return the weapons with which the British had equipped it. Chin Peng, who acted as the liaison officer with the

British, carried out this task in good faith and with good humor, up to a point, and made more British friends in doing so. At impressive ceremonies, the uniformed guerrillas turned in their weapons; each received a campaign medal and 300 Malayan dollars ($100 U.S.) for his services. The number of weapons handed in was, in fact, more than the British had delivered. In the confusion of the British defeat in 1942, thousands of British weapons and much ammunition had been lying about for the taking, not only in the big depots but also in the small police armories and troop positions that had been overrun. The Japanese soldiers, pressing urgently forward to outflank the next position, had not encumbered themselves with these weapons; and the Chinese guerrillas had helped themselves at leisure. Besides the weapons handed in, therefore, the Communists had large stocks of arms and ammunition concealed in the jungle, ready to re-equip their eight guerrilla regiments when necessary.

The Malayan People's Anti-Japanese Army also established an "Old Comrades' Association," with branches in every town. Its ostensible aim was to look after the welfare of the ex-guerrilla fighters, but its real purpose was to keep the regiments alive in shadow form, with company commanders, commissars, riflemen, and couriers listed and ready to rally to arms. At the same time, they made sure that their people's organization among the squatters and villagers was maintained through the parallel hierarchy.

At this stage, the British Government introduced a new constitution for Malaya that was to prove an unhappy failure—the so-called Malayan Union. Except in the three British-governed settlements of Singapore, Malacca, and Penang, the Chinese and Indian Malayans had no say in running their states, which the nine Malay Sultans governed with the aid of British advisers. The Malayan Union envisaged Malaya as a single entity, a parliamentary democracy established on the British model, with a view to independence. The Chinese and Indians were to gain the vote and equal rights; and the Sultans would become merely regional community and religious leaders of the Malays. This seemed reasonable to policy planners in London. Unfortunately, the only Malayans enthusiastic about the idea in 1946 were the prosperous Chinese businessmen, most of whom were also supporters of the Kuomintang. For this reason, the Malayan Communist Party was against it; the Party

# FIGURE 1
## Malaya

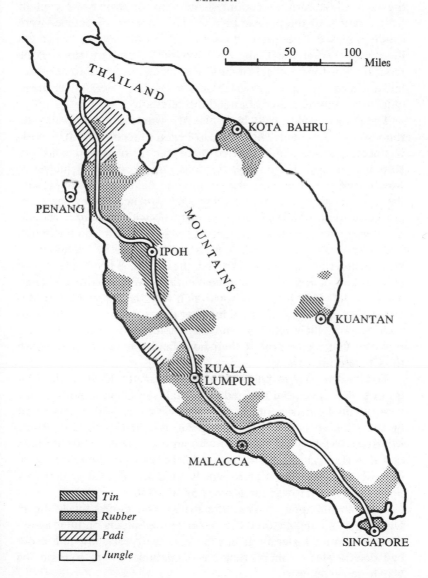

also knew that any strengthening of the central government would make a Communist takeover more difficult. The remaining Chinese and Indians (the small shopkeepers and traders, particularly) gave the idea a lukewarm reception, since many of them were content with a return to the prewar regime. The Malays, of course, were solidly opposed. They were, however, given little chance to express their views. After less than seven months of military rule by the reoccupation forces, the British Government inaugurated the Malayan Union in April, 1946. Not one Malay ruler, government official, or representative attended the ceremony.

The British could hardly have picked a worse moment to alienate the Malays. The country had scarcely begun to recover from its postwar economic and administrative chaos; the Chinese were split into Kuomintang and Communist factions, the unrulier elements of which were indulging increasingly in gang fights and holdups; and there was a wave of ordinary crime and violence among the teenage generation, which had been brought up without proper schooling during the Japanese occupation. Many British administrators had died in Japanese prison camps, and the hastily recruited replacements were inexperienced. At the working level, the public officials and policemen were almost entirely Malay. Already somewhat shamefaced over their cooperation with the Japanese, the Malays were now deeply affronted by what they regarded as an insult to their Sultans, their religion, and their community; and they were resentful that the control of their homeland was to be shared with the Chinese immigrants.

Today, it is easy to point out that most of the ideas of the Malayan Union have been realized. The Malayan Chinese do have the vote as equal citizens; and in the 1963 elections, with a large part of the Chinese community voting for the first time, the Prime Minister, a Malay, was returned with an even greater majority than in 1959. Radical reforms of an established society, however, work best when allowed to mature slowly; and racial rivalry, certainly not dead even yet, was far too strong in 1946.

After an unhappy struggle, the British abandoned the Malayan Union in 1948 and restored the power of the Sultans on their agreement to form a Federation; but in those two years, law and order had deteriorated so much that the Communists were well on the way to seizing power.

# 3

# STRIKES AND SUBVERSION

I N 1946–47, the Malayan Communist Party was aiming to take control of the government by following the classic Russian pattern, in which the revolutionaries first attempt to disrupt the economy so that the daily life of the people goes from bad to worse. Confidence in the government deteriorates, and in the interests of national unity the government is persuaded to allow left-wing parties (including Communists, or Communists under another name) to join a coalition; the Communists soon have control of key departments. This is all quite legal and overt. At the same time, the Party is intensifying its undercover activities to infiltrate a network of selected and trained Communists into positions where they can influence people and events at every level. Czechoslovakia was the classic example of this.

Communist subversion had been going on for many years in Malaya. It was still being conducted through many channels, of which three were of particular importance: the front organizations, the Chinese schools, and the trade unions.

Many clubs for young Chinese were dominated and guided by the Malayan Communist Party in 1946.[1] There was little need for them to conceal their Communist affiliation because the MCP was legal and had acquired great prestige from its leadership of the resistance against the Japanese. Among themselves, the members talked freely of ousting the British. The boys and girls, however, were attracted more by social factors than by politics. Life after the war seemed drab and lacking in purpose, even for the children of quite prosperous Chinese. When they found a group of lively young people, they wanted to join it.

The Communists used the front organizations primarily to test and select leaders. New members soon became aware that the people they most admired in the club had Marxist beliefs, and the wish to emulate them as leaders was often followed by a wish to emulate them as Marxists. Those youths who showed promise might be Party members within a year.

Communists also were active in Chinese schools, which were attended by many persons in their early twenties, as well as teen-agers, because the schools had been closed during the war. It was from these older pupils that the Communists recruited their leaders to spread propaganda, select promising material, and exploit grievances.

There were many grievances to exploit. The chief ones were the preference given to Malays in selection for government posts and the denial of full citizenship rights to the Chinese. Although the Chinese in practice seldom sought government posts, preferring commerce, it was not difficult to convince Chinese students that they would be second-class citizens until the Communist Party was in power.

There was also the language question. The only common language in Malaya was English. Not only did each of the three main races have its own language, but the Chinese themselves spoke many tongues. Teaching at the University of Malaya was—and still is—in English; and in the Chinese middle and senior schools, for

---

[1] For a good account of Communist methods of subversion at this time, see Lucian W. Pye, *Guerrilla Communism in Malaya,* chap. ii.

boys and girls preparing for the university, English played a dominant part. Among the young, intensely race-conscious Chinese, this was a sore point.

The Communists had another good reason for choosing the schools as a target: When the time comes to use the riot weapon, students provide admirably inflammable material. There is no better means to promote bitterness than the sight of a big policeman beating up a boy half his size. Or, better still, a girl.

Trade unions are always a prime target for Communist subversion because strikes are powerful weapons against a government.

Subversion in the Malayan unions was based on the same technique used in the clubs. The Communists picked out natural leaders from among the workers and attracted them into personal friendships and group activities in which they could be tested and won over. Then they were encouraged to volunteer for election to the grass-roots union post of shop steward. Once elected, they were taught how to win concessions from management for their fellow workers and establish themselves as popular champions.

From this base, the Communists attempted to control in turn the branch, district, regional, and national executive committees of the unions. But here they ran into difficulty. In trade unions that have been allowed to develop under Communist guidance, the higher committees are elected by representatives from the stage below and the Communists have only to get their men in as shop stewards to gain control of the entire organization. The Malayan unions were modeled on their British counterparts, however, in which the branch committees must be elected by a general meeting.

Even this safeguard, however, is not foolproof. It is not easy to attract men away from their recreational activities to attend union meetings after work, so quorums are necessarily small. This gives the Communists their chance, for they go to great pains to mobilize their supporters, count heads, and pick their moment for a snap vote. By this means they get their man in as secretary, and it thereafter becomes easier to rig future meetings to elect the rest of the committee—and so on up the line, until they have control of the whole union hierarchy up to the national executive.

Although the Communists had not gained control of the national executives of individual unions in Malaya, they had taken advantage of the postwar chaos to form a Communist-dominated Pan-

Malayan Federation of Trade Unions. Through this, they were able to disrupt the whole country with a general strike in 1947. Two things brought the strike to an end: the lack of union funds for strike pay and the government's power to banish anyone not a Malayan citizen—and this included most of the Chinese Communists. The police had the names of the leaders of the Pan-Malayan Federation, and the Communists shrank from provoking the government to drastic action at this stage.

Even so, they overplayed their hand by organizing more than 300 major strikes in 1947.[2] The government was forced to pass three very effective pieces of legislation in May, 1948. The first was an ordinance requiring all union officers except the secretary to have three years' experience in the trade concerned. This barred most of the professional Communists who were directing activities from the top. Many others were barred by the second ordinance, which excluded men convicted of intimidation, extortion, and various other crimes. The third outlawed all federations not composed of unions in allied trades. This put an end to the Pan-Malayan Federation itself.

If the Communists hoped to whip up a public outcry against these measures, they were disappointed. The unions' rank-and-file members were fed up with strikes, and the non-Communist union executives were exasperated with the Pan-Malayan Federation's interference in their affairs. The government measures were received tolerantly and even with relief, and the Communists' campaign of strikes was brought to an end.

This also marked the end of their attempt to gain power in Malaya by "legal" means. A new policy edict had just gone out from a Moscow-sponsored conference of Asian Communist parties in Calcutta, which resolved that the time was ripe for the "armed struggle" to be launched all over Asia. The next two years were to bring massive successes to Communist armies. Mao Tse-tung's army was already overrunning China. Ho Chi Minh's would soon be ready to seize the frontier forts in North Vietnam. And violence was to break out in full force in Malaya.

---

[2] Harry Miller, *The Communist Menace in Malaya*, p. 74.

# 4

# RIOT AND REBELLION

**E**ARLY in "the Year of Strikes," 1947, circumstances finally caught up with Lai Tek, the Secretary General of the Malayan Communist Party. Certain Communists openly accused Lai Tek of wartime collaboration with the Japanese. Some members of the MCP's Central Executive Committee were dissatisfied with his leadership. Allegedly on the advice of Mao Tse-tung's representative (but conceivably because he still had some contact with the British Special Branch), Lai Tek seemed content to work for power through constitutional means—a damning "rightist" heresy in the eyes of the true Communist. He was also personally disliked and distrusted by some of his colleagues.

The storm against Lai Tek broke at a meeting of the Central Executive Committee in February, 1947. His opponents clashed with a faction still loyal, and the meeting ended in uproar. A rendezvous was fixed for the next meeting, two weeks later. Lai Tek did not show up, and he has never been seen since. Nor have the Party funds. His fate remains a mystery.

His successor was Chin Peng, elected Secretary General at twenty-six. Chin Peng headed a Party committed to seize power from the British but still attempting to do it by legal means of strikes, peaceful demonstrations, and subversion. Within a year, the campaign shifted to open violence in two forms—raids and sabotage by armed units and riots by mainly unarmed crowds.

The Communist-directed raids in Malaya, as elsewhere, involved murdering government officials, intimidating their collaborators, and sabotaging the government's movement of security forces and its administration of the daily life of the country. The raids in 1948 seemed to the public to be merely an intensification of the activities of the unruly Chinese Communist and Kuomintang factions, known as "bandit gangs." In fact, however, the gangs were reactivated units of the Malayan People's Anti-Japanese Army, now renamed the Malayan People's Anti-British Army. At first, the men lived in their villages and formed for raids as required, but they were soon to find it necessary to operate from the jungle.

Rioting in Malaya was less widespread than in most revolutions because the police were efficient and troops to support them were deployed promptly. But periodic rioting continued throughout the war, and the riots in Singapore in 1956 and Ipoh in 1957 were two of the most dangerous. Their context was different from the riots of 1947–48, but their conduct and control were similar; so here I draw on the experiences of these later ones to throw light on the earlier events. Riot and riot-control techniques vary much less than other forms of insurgency, and what was right in Russia in 1917 is likely also be to be right in Africa or Asia in the 1960's.

The Communist pattern is to exploit real or imaginary grievances, bring about clashes between the police and the public, and thereby poison relations between them. Where possible, the circumstances are stage-managed so that not only is the public sense of justice outraged, but the individual policemen and soldiers themselves begin to doubt the rightness of their actions and to sympathize with the crowd. The fostering of this feeling of fraternity is well described by Trotsky in his account of the rioting in Petrograd in February, 1917.[1]

---

[1] Leon Trotsky, *The Russian Revolution,* trans. Max Eastman (New York: Doubleday Anchor Books, 1959), pp. 97–128.

The revolutionaries at this stage are not mainly concerned to change the system of government. Their aim is to seize the reins of the existing system by putting Communists in the ministries, police headquarters, radio station, and telephone office. Their hope is that by murder, intimidation, and constant disorder the morale of public officials will be so worn down that they will (like the Russian officials in Petrograd in 1917) sit dejectedly at their telephones, aware of the noise outside and of what it implies, but without the courage or the will to act. In the rising chaos, the Communists can oust them with little resistance, and the people are in a mood to rally to any strong man or party that seems to be in control and to have a plan for restoring order.

Professional revolutionaries must get more exasperated with crowds than with any of their other tools. Crowds are difficult to mobilize and, once launched, almost impossible to control. They are fickle, since a large part of them usually have just come along to watch. A trifling incident resulting in blood on a child's face may rouse them to fury. Something else may just as easily dissolve them into laughter. A British officer serving with the Malayan police told how he once found himself facing a mass of hostile Chinese. Unable to think what to do, he seized one of their conical straw hats and threw it high into the air. This was so unexpected that it delighted the Chinese. Other hats began soaring up and down like a flock of flying saucers, and the crisis was past.

A main problem for the Communists in postwar Malaya was to find a time and place at which a demonstration was likely to attract a crowd in a proper mood to clash with the police. This is one reason why rioting was most commonly based on a strike or the closing of a school. The crowds would be there, they would consist mostly of people concerned, and they would have nothing else to do. Thus, as well as leading strikes, the Communists frequently tried to bring about such indiscipline in a school that the authorities were tempted to close it for a period. The Communists, who had until then kept well in the background, would be ready to exploit the situation.

The Communists made every effort to involve Chinese schoolgirls with the police. Chinese girls are tough and determined, and they are also small. During the 1957 riots in Ipoh, a number of British police officers were still employed by the newly independent

Malayan Government; their orders were to keep in the background in order not to hand the Communists a propaganda gift. They did— until a young British Special Branch officer in plain clothes saw a Malay policewoman being viciously beaten by six tough Chinese girls. A Chinese crowd was obviously enjoying the show. The officer waded in and stopped the beating. Almost every paper next morning published a dramatic picture of the white man holding a struggling girl with his left arm and raising his right arm to strike her. The picture did not show the marks where she had just sunk her teeth into his left hand, nor did it show the other five girls or the battered Malay policewoman.

Was he right to intervene? Undoubtedly he was, because if he had done nothing the effect, both on the police and on the crowd, would have been still worse. Of course, the policewoman should not have been allowed to be so isolated and exposed, but such situations are bound to occur, and the skill of the instigators of a riot lies in creating circumstances in which they do.

Prevention of riots, like almost everything else in counterinsurgency, depends primarily on good intelligence and imaginative interpretation of it. Intelligence is easier to acquire at this stage than at any other, because whether the riots develop from demonstrations, strikes, or lockouts, none of these occur without a large number of people knowing in advance. The government's task is to maintain paid informers in every block. This, however, costs money and requires a large Special Branch staff to organize it. Riots occur mainly in the early stages of the revolutionary spectrum, when governments are often either complacent, reluctant to spend money, or taken off guard.

The best riot-prevention organization in my experience was not in Malaya, but in Trieste in 1946–47, when the Yugoslav Communists were attempting to seize the city from the Allied forces that had reoccupied it. The racial situation was one of those in which there could be no "fair" solution. The rural area for miles around was Yugoslav, but in the midst of it, the Italians had created this thriving city and port in which the population was overwhelmingly Italian—except in one almost wholly Yugoslav quarter in the northern part of the city. The Communists were instigating these

Yugoslavs to make demonstrations in the hope that clashes with the police and the Allied soldiers would eventually bring such chaos that the Italians would despair of running this enclave in a hostile area, and agree to surrender it to "neutral" control. A state of emergency was declared, and the right to assemble for demonstrations was suspended. Our brigade was sent down from Germany to help keep control, and my squadron was quartered in an old barracks in the Yugoslav quarter. The police, locally recruited but under British officers, had built up a good network of informers. There was only a limited number of open city squares, playing fields, etc., in which demonstrations could form up. When word got to the Yugoslavs in their tenements to rally at one of these, within a few moments this news was telephoned to police headquarters by informers. The first line of support was a U.S. Constabulary Battalion especially organized for the task. Within minutes, jeeploads of white-helmeted GI's would be parked with NO ENTRY signs on every approach to the square concerned. The crowd on each approach would be a small one, unaware that others were converging from other directions. They could see, however, that the security forces were already on the spot, and clearly prepared to use force if necessary. This was enough to make all but the most militant lose heart and return home. The few who did infiltrate to the square were greeted by a train of U.S. Army jeeps driving fast around the perimeter with night sticks flailing like knives on a Roman chariot wheel. In the six months that we were there, not a single effective crowd for a riot was able even to assemble, still less to get under way toward the city center.

Almost as important as good intelligence is a plan for manning vulnerable points quickly, before the rioters can reach them, and for reinforcing those that are threatened. Since there are seldom enough police or troops to man all of them, careful judgment is needed to decide how many can be manned strongly enough to be held until the reinforcements arrive, and which these are to be. In this respect, it is worth looking at the list of targets compiled by the father of all riot chiefs of staff—Trotsky in Petrograd in 1917: the railroad stations, the lighting plant, the munition and food stores, the waterworks, the (key) bridge, the Telephone Exchange, the State Bank, the big printing-plants . . . the Telegraph Station and the Post Office.[2] Any list today would be headed by the radio and television stations and would include gasoline depots and bus stations, but otherwise Trotsky's list is as good as any. To support their *coup d'état,* the Bolsheviks had persuaded the crew of a naval cruiser on the river and the soldiers in a key fortress to mutiny; but Trotsky's list included all they planned to seize. They accomplished these seizures; and although the administration still held all government offices, army headquarters, police stations—and indeed virtually all the rest of Russia—Trotsky was able to announce (and held the means to announce) that the Bolsheviks had taken over the government.

In controlling riots, it is unwise to substitute soldiers for policemen if it can be avoided. Nevertheless, British troops are now trained, and often have to be used, to disperse crowds. We are careful, however, not to give in to the inevitable requests from hard-pressed policemen to dissipate all the soldiers to guard vulnerable points, leaving none to reinforce those actually attacked or to deal with major riots when they occur. When our soldiers operate as police, they are equipped as police, with shields and night sticks or pistols rather than rifles, and use police tactics, with baton charges and tear gas. It is most undesirable for soldiers armed with rifles to come into bodily contact with a hostile crowd, since the rifles may be seized. Soldiers carrying rifles should be kept in recognizable military formations and handled so that the crowd is left in no doubt that they will shoot to kill if the need arises.

Picking the right moment to commit soldiers in a military role requires sound judgment. In some cases, a quick and visible deployment of troops in strength may nip trouble in the bud. On the other hand, if violence has already begun, it is better to keep troops out of sight until the crowd seems ready to take an action that the troops must prevent at any cost; for example, overrunning a telephone exchange or radio station. If troops appear prematurely and the crowd gets away with its next step without drawing fire, it is likely to be encouraged to go further.

The Singapore riots of 1956 offered a good example of both these aspects. The Communists, who were losing ground badly in the jungle war, decided to try to disrupt the port of Singapore,

---

[2] *Ibid.,* p. 359.

through which virtually all supplies for Malaya were channeled. Exploiting a labor dispute, they engineered a general strike. The police learned of their plans the day before, and within twenty-four hours, six battalions of infantry were pulled out of the jungle (nearly a third of the counterguerrilla army) and poured across the causeway to the island. Large crowds were already assembling, but word of the army's quick and massive reinforcement had an immediate sobering effect. Thereafter, five of the battalions were kept out of sight, though everyone knew they were in the city. Only one battalion was deployed, and only one of its detachments had to open fire. The most potentially dangerous riot in the whole insurgency was stifled with virtually no bloodshed, and the troops were back in the jungle within three days.

The riots instigated by the Communists in 1948 were not dealt with so promptly, and although they were far smaller and less dangerous than in 1956, many more people were killed. For example, in the first week of June, 1948, 7 were killed and 10 wounded in a riot involving only 200 people. The atmosphere of bitterness and defiance was growing.

At this stage, Chin Peng decided to remobilize the guerrilla army. The men on the Old Comrades' roll of the MPAJA were ordered to report to jungle camps, where arms and ammunition awaited them. With the guerrillas under the training and discipline of their officers, the raids became more effective. They were increasingly concentrated on specific targets—mostly British plantation managers and British and Malay public officials. Laborers who failed to support strikes were shot; and posters appeared all over Malaya exhorting workers to kill their British employers, to kill those who "worked for other races," and to kill those who were "running dogs for the police."

On June 17, 1948, the High Commissioner, under strong pressure from the representatives of all races in the Federal Legislative Council, declared a state of emergency. The anti-Communist war in Malaya had officially begun.

# 5

# A STATE OF EMERGENCY

A STATE of emergency is quite different from martial law. Under martial law, the civil government recognizes that the situation is beyond its control and orders the army to take over. Army colonels assume the government of provinces and cities, give orders to the police, and operate (if need be with soldiers) the essential public utilities and transport. Criminals are tried by military courts and subject to military punishments. The army, in fact, governs the country.

That, in Malaya, was never the case. The civil government—federal, state, district, and village—exercised control throughout. The army acted in their support and always under their direction. The method of this direction, which developed as the war progressed, will be described in later chapters. The provisions of the state of emergency gave legal backing to actions foreseen as necessary by soldiers, police, and government officials to control violence, to prevent the sustenance of the armed Communist units, and to find and capture or kill them.

The Emergency Regulations were special laws passed by the Federal Legislature in June, 1948. As revised in 1949 and amended in 1953, they ran to 149 pages, covering subjects as diverse as possession of firearms, powers of arrest and detention, control of food supplies, and clearing of undergrowth. The detail they cover may seem surprising, but in fighting an insurgency of this kind, it is vital that every action by government officials, policemen, and soldiers be strictly within the law. The law can be as tough as is needed, provided that it is properly enacted and that officials are manifestly subject to it themselves.

The most important measure called for the entire population over twelve years old to register at the police stations, where copies of their photographs and thumbprints were made. One copy was placed on an identity card to be carried by the registrant; another was retained at the police station. Many unsuspected Communists, reluctant to have their photographs and thumbprints recorded on police files, first drew suspicion on themselves by failing to report for registration. More important, registration hampered all Communist movement and activity, despite efforts to disrupt the system by terror, wholesale destruction of identity cards, and forgery.

In the most effective use of the registration powers, police set up cordons at early morning and screened everyone in a village. Anyone who should not have been there was picked up, and anyone whose absence could not be explained satisfactorily was thereafter a particular target for police surveillance.

Workers in the rubber and paddy fields at first were asked to produce their identity cards before going into the fields and to carry the cards on the job. But these workers became special targets for the guerrillas, who tore up the identity cards and threatened the bearers with death if they registered again. The government reacted effectively by collecting the identity cards and issuing tallies instead as the workers went out to the fields. The tallies were handed back in exchange for the identity cards on return. If the Communists stole the tally, it was only a minor nuisance for the owner to re-establish his identity at the police station and to reclaim his card.

No identity-card system will work (as indeed it has failed to work in South Vietnam) unless the holder has a real incentive to look after his own card. In Malaya, the identity card was needed to obtain a food ration, space in a resettled village, a grant to build on it, an extra patch for growing vegetables, and many other things. The registration system, as expected, was not popular; but the people soon realized that life with identity cards was easier than life without them, so they took good care of theirs.

Outside the villages, the need for an identity card (or a tally) prevented guerrillas in disguise from moving about freely on the rubber estates and the roads; and their clandestine couriers found it more difficult to deliver messages. Anyone found by a police check to be outside his normal neighborhood without a convincing explanation would attract special attention in the future, and it was from shreds of evidence such as these that intelligence was built up and agents recruited to betray the Communists.

The system had its greatest effect inside the villages, however, because it became almost impossible for guerrillas to live among the people. It truly separated the guerrillas from the people. This is the prime requisite in defeating a guerrilla insurgency; it gives the people protection and forces the guerrillas to make prearranged contacts with their supporters. Such contacts provide the most fruitful field for the intelligence that kills.

Second in importance only to registration was the power to arrest and detain without trial. This is a suspension of what all free countries rightly regard as a basic human right—the right of habeas corpus. The suspension can be abused, and even in the best supervised police forces, this is sometimes bound to occur. It increases opposition to the government and provides the enemy with a major propaganda weapon. All the same, it is essential in fighting any serious Communist insurgency because Communist leaders seldom act in the open or make themselves liable to conviction, and because the Communist techniques for intimidation are so well developed that few witnesses dare to give evidence against them, even in closed court. The police thus often possess unanswerable evidence against an offender but cannot convict. If this were not so, the stage would never have been reached for a state of emergency to become necessary.

Careful safeguards are needed, and Malaya had a Public Review Board made up of independent citizens who examined each case at regular intervals (once a year at first, but later every six months) and heard appeals. The regulations governing detention, review, and appeals were widely published; and proceedings were conducted as openly as security allowed.

Another necessary emergency power was the right to search private property without a warrant. This again is the suspension of a basic freedom, and history is full of examples of its abuse. As with the power of detention, however, it is in the end more acceptable if it is formally and publicly passed as legislation, rather than imposed without proper authority by individual policemen. The snap checks of villages and the capture of fugitives would have been impossible without it.

Imposition of the death sentence for a man caught with an unauthorized weapon became mandatory for judges. The sentence could be commuted; or, if the arrested person were prepared to assist the police in capturing others, he might never be charged with the offense at all.

Anyone convicted of knowingly possessing Communist documents or assisting Communist propaganda was liable to imprisonment for ten years.

The power to impose curfews was flexible. They could be imposed to suit the circumstances—in cities in disorder, in rural villages, or rubber estates, or as a collective punishment in an area where the people were persistently supporting the guerrillas.

People often express surprise that the Malayan Communist Party and its front organizations were not declared illegal until July 23, 1948, but there was sense in this. An open Communist Party invariably operates in two spheres. It has its "legal" or overt sphere, in which it issues propaganda, fosters strikes and demonstrations, and acts as a normal political party. In the "illegal" or clandestine sphere, however, it operates whether the Party is open or proscribed, by subversion, intimidation, terror, extortion, and robbery. These go on all the time. So long as the Party is legal, the police have some overt targets to watch—Party headquarters, newspaper offices, meetings. And, although as far as possible most of the "illegal" workers are instructed to avoid such public appearances, there are inevitable contacts between overt and covert members, in homes, parks, streets, cafés. By trailing the legal workers, the police get leads into the clandestine sphere that could not be obtained if there were no legal operations. In July, 1948, it clearly became necessary to proscribe the Party to enforce the Emergency Regulations. The police arrested 600 known Party members in an initial sweep (though many more had already taken to the jungle), and the police blacklists would have been far shorter if the Party had been illegal for the previous three years.

Many other Emergency Regulations did not have their effect until the insurgency had progressed from open violence in 1948–49 to clandestine terror in the villages in the 1950's. These will be discussed in context. The more important ones covered the right to shoot on sight in prohibited areas, an essential provision for patrols operating in jungle terrain; resettlement, i.e., the right to direct individuals to live in or move out of specified places; and food control, including the death penalty for anyone convicted of demanding supplies for the guerrillas and imprisonment for anyone giving in to these demands.

No regulations, however sound, can achieve results without effective local government. Where this is lacking, the regulations may do more harm than good, since inequitable enforcement brings resentment and nonenforcement brings contempt.

The Malayan Federation is divided into states; the states are divided into districts (similar in size to U.S. counties). In 1948, the Federation had a British High Commissioner (the Governor); each state was ruled by a Malay Sultan aided by a number of British and Malayan officials. The district officers were mainly British.

It is at the village level, however, that local government becomes a decisive factor in counterinsurgency; and officials at this level were virtually 100 per cent Malayan throughout the conflict. The local government was based on elected town and village councils, supported by Malayan police and officials for public health, information, resettlement, education, etc., as appropriate, depending on the town's size. As in Vietnam, these officials became major targets for Communist terror. A few officials, of course, were apathetic, easily intimidated, or treacherous, but the great majority were stanch and loyal. Most were Malays or Indians who had no love either for the Chinese or for Communism, but even they could never have survived if they had not been effectively protected by the village police posts.

Emergency measures for population control always come later than they should, for very good reasons. In Malaya, the village police posts were not brought up to viable strength until 1949; and the government was criticized for failing to introduce the Emergency Regulations until June, 1948. It is true that the lives lost in May and June, 1948, might have been saved. Sadly, however, such drastic legislation would never have been accepted by the public until those lives had been lost; it would merely have provoked unrest in which more lives would have been lost in the end.

I was not in Malaya in 1948. If I had been, I would probably share the bitterness of those who were there, particularly the British rubber planters who saw one out of every ten of their number killed before effective action was taken. I doubt, however, if the state of emergency could have been declared much earlier.

Chin Peng's decision to recall the Communist army to the jungle undoubtedly saved him and many other known Communists from arrest under the Emergency Regulations. This may have been pure luck, dictated by the need to mobilize his army for training and more effective action; or it may be that he suspected that the state of emergency was coming and recalled his men to preclude their arrest. Whatever his reasons, the Emergency Regulations would in any case have forced the Communists to take to the jungle, particularly those regulations providing for detention without trial and for compulsory registration of the population. Although the guerrillas had a flying start, the Emergency Regulations not only kept them in the jungle but also provided the ground rules under which they were to be beaten.

# 6

# THE BIG BATTALIONS

IN spite of the declaration of the state of emergency, there is no doubt that in the first nine months of the war, the Communists had a chance to establish a position from which it would have been very difficult to dislodge them. The country was in no way geared for the enforcement of the Emergency Regulations, and the balance of forces was more in the Communists' favor than it was ever to be again.

In June, 1948, the Communist regiments had already been mobilized in the jungle. Their underground organizations in the villages, well practiced from the MPAJA days, were ready to supply them. Opposing them at this time were 10 infantry battalions (2 British, 5 Gurkha, and 3 Malay) and 9,000 police. The balance of infantry soldiers and armed guerrillas *in the jungle* was, in fact, remarkably even; and it remained so for the next three years.

Much nonsense is heard on the subject of tie-down ratios in

guerrilla warfare—that 10 to 12 government troops are needed to tie down a single guerrilla, for instance. This is a dangerous illusion, arising from a disregard for the facts. It is quite true that, if the total figures of armed policemen and soldiers are balanced against armed guerrillas in any such war, the difference is large. This does not, however, represent the difference *in the jungle,* for three reasons: first, because a large part of the army consists of "overheads"—men concerned with command, control, supply, support, and road and air movement, who wear uniforms but never go into the jungle; second, because, though some of these overheads may be luxuries, others (such as command and supply) are provided for the guerrillas as well, not by uniformed men but by the Party organization and the supporters in the villages, who are numbered not in thousands but in hundreds of thousands; and third, because the protection and control of these villages ties up large numbers of policemen who, like so many of the soldiers, do not go into the jungle but are necessary all the same.

An infantry battalion in Malaya had about 700 men; but, as in the U.S. Army, or any other regular army, a substantial number of these were drivers, cooks, clerks, signalers, or members of the quartermaster staff. A battalion does well to put 400 riflemen into the field. Thus the 10 battalions in Malaya in 1948 could field at the most 4,000 riflemen for patrols and operations against the 4,000 guerrillas in the jungle. By 1951, the strength had risen to 20 battalions (8,000 riflemen), but by then the guerrillas also had 8,000 men.

Thereafter, the government's position began to improve in almost every respect. In 1948, a large proportion of the soldiers had been tied down as static guards and escorts because there were not enough police for these duties. By 1951, the police not only were able to take over these duties but also formed their own jungle squads; and later, the Police Field Force, 3,000 strong, manned the deep jungle forts in the aborigine areas. By the turning point of the war (1952), the effective *jungle* strength of the army and police together probably reached a 2-to-1 superiority over the guerrillas; but it was never anywhere near the 10- or 12-to-1 ratio so often quoted by commentators. The power of the army lay not in its over-all superiority but in its flexibility: In defense, it was able to react quickly to guerrilla raids; in offense, it was able to concentrate large numbers of small patrols and ambushes in single districts one after the other.

The main task of the police force was in the populated areas. The rural Chinese population was more than 1 million. Of these perhaps 60,000 were active organizers of Communist support in the villages and squatter areas, using the knife and the hatchet rather than the gun to coerce this support. Up to 500,000 (some say more) succumbed to this leadership and worked, willingly or unwillingly, for the Communists. It is against these figures, and not against the numbers of guerrillas in the jungle, that police strength must be compared. The 9,000 constables available in June, 1948, had no hope whatever of protecting their people or preventing them from contacting the guerrillas. Within six months, however, the 9,000 had risen to nearly 50,000; and later, these were supplemented by a part-time Home Guard, of whom 40,000 could be expected to be on duty at any time. Thus, at the peak of the emergency, there was perhaps 1 policeman or home guardsman for every 5 active or 10 potential *supporters* for the guerrillas. In 1948, however, there was less than 1 for every 100.

Chin Peng's plan in essence was the same as Ho Chi Minh's, following the teaching of Mao Tse-tung. Basing himself in the jungle, he hoped first to "liberate" the rubber estates along its fringes; he knew he could rely on the squatters living there. Then he hoped to extend his control into the neighboring villages until he had an area in which he could establish a people's republic and to which he could bring his guerrillas from the jungle to be trained and equipped for big battles in the open. The final stage would be to challenge and beat the British-Malayan Government Army in conventional warfare, as Mao was doing triumphantly in North China and as Ho Chi Minh was shortly to do at Dien Bien Phu.

Chin Peng's plan, however, retained a certain flavor of the original Russian pattern. He hoped that the areas to be liberated would fall into his hands through popular risings rather than by the patient extermination or neutralization of government control on which he was to embark later.

Thus, in 1948, the guerrillas continued to concentrate their efforts on sabotage and violence designed to reduce the country to chaos so that the people would rally to the Communist parallel hierarchy as the best hope of restoring order. By the end of 1948, the guerrillas had killed 900 people (more civilians than soldiers); but in these critical months, their hopes of a general rising faded. By April, 1949, they realized that they must revise their plans.

The likeliest explanation of this error of judgment is that the Malayan Communist leaders, almost all of whom were city bourgeois, assumed that rural Malaya would react as rural China had reacted. There were, however, tremendous differences. First, rural China's economy was based on subsistence agriculture, but Malaya grows only a third of its own food. Even in the rural areas, most of the Malayan Chinese earn their living as rubber tappers or tin miners. Thus, the peasants in China had nothing to lose; but a collapse of the rubber and tin industries in Malaya would bring a large part of the rural population to the brink of starvation, and this was fresh in their minds from the Japanese occupation.

Secondly, rural China is generally fertile and teeming with people; but 80 per cent of Malaya is jungle, inhabited only by a handful of primitive seminomadic aborigines. Due to the Emergency Regulations, it was in the jungle that the Communist guerrilla army was initially forced to live. The Malayan jungle is rough and mountainous, rising to more than 7,000 feet. It is so dense in places (particularly near the fringes) that a patrol may take four hours to cover a mile, and it can pass within 5 yards of a man or within 50 yards of a 100-man camp without knowing it. The remaining 20 per cent of the surface of the country, mainly on the western side of the central mountain spine, has been cleared of jungle, generally in a strip 5 to 10 miles wide, extending 500 miles from the border of Thailand to the island of Singapore. This strip contains the bulk of the rubber plantations and tin mines, with a certain amount of paddy and tapioca in the north and oil palm and pineapple in the south. A tarmac highway and a railroad run down the strip to carry the rubber and tin to Singapore for export. Like Britain, Malaya depends on exports for her prosperity.

Because the rubber and tin are worked almost entirely by the Chinese and Indians, and because the Malays' agricultural kampongs (villages) are generally set apart, most of the villages astride the road through the rubber and tin areas are wholly Indian or Chinese. It was around these Chinese villages that the war was fought.

In 1948, however, at least half the rural Chinese population did not live in the villages at all. It was mainly on the 423,000 squatters, still living on the jungle fringes to which so many had fled during the Japanese occupation, that the Communist jungle army in 1948–50 depended for supplies and information.

The eight regiments of the Malayan People's Anti-British Army were organized as in the anti-Japanese days. They lived in large camps, normally of company size. These were well-appointed, with parade grounds and classrooms in which the soldiers spent more than half their time, attending political indoctrination and self-criticism sessions, lectures on current affairs, and classes in Mandarin Chinese. Relatively few of the men had been honored by election to the Communist Party; indeed, the proportion of Party members never exceeded 30 per cent in the jungle and was far lower among the squatters and the supporters in the villages.

Undoubtedly, when the guerrillas went into the jungle in 1948, there was a sharp rise in their morale; many were MPAJA veterans, and they were trusted to the extent of regular home leaves. Later, as they were joined by new draftees, many of whom were criminals or misfits from ordinary life, their privileges had to be withdrawn, and morale deteriorated steadily. After scarcely more than a year in action, many of these unreliable elements were to surrender under the first amnesty offer; but the hard core remained, and some of them are with Chin Peng to this day.

The regiments operated in the early days mainly in the company groups in which they lived, though there were also smaller raids and a number of larger ones involving 200 or 300 men. These raids inflicted a considerable amount of permanent damage to rubber trees and tin mines. Even though many of the Chinese had some sympathy with the jungle army, they saw no point in joining in destroying the rubber trees and tin mines—the only means they would ever have of earning a living, whether under the British or the Communists. The guerrilla regiments were losing a growing number of men in clashes with soldiers on the jungle fringe, and there were increasing numbers of attacks on their camps by infantry companies that trailed them back into the jungle after their raids.

In April, 1949, the charts in the police stations began to show a sharp fall in the number of guerrilla incidents—murders, raids, slashings of rubber trees, and burning of tin-mine pumping stations.

The Emergency Regulations were getting into their stride; and, with many more policemen and soldiers to be seen, including three battalions of well-disciplined guardsmen fresh from London, many people leaped to the false conclusion that the emergency was under control. In fact, the Communists had withdrawn their regiments deep into the jungle to reorganize and make a new plan. They had realized that they could not get control of any "liberated area" unless they first systematically destroyed local government in the villages, and in particular, the police posts. They had discovered, with some bitterness, that the Malayan Chinese masses were depressingly lacking in revolutionary fervor when it came to a choice between sacrifices for the new order and full stomachs for their families.

However, the Communists still harbored the illusion that the people in their hearts really wanted revolution, that all they needed was firm, uncompromising leadership. Chin Peng's new plan, therefore, was to strengthen the organizations that worked among the people so that he could be sure of getting supplies to sustain him through what he now realized would be a long war.

Meanwhile, in the rather naïve hope of winning wider support from the Malays and Indians, the army was again renamed. It became the Malayan Races' Liberation Army (MRLA); and the leaders set about retraining it for the task of destroying the structure of local government, village by village, by what the French in Indochina came to call the "oil-spot technique"—the oil spots linking up into a patch, and the patches into an area big enough to justify a claim for world recognition of a *de facto* people's republic.

An oil spot, however, cannot develop unless the village police post is neutralized.

In October, 1949, after a six-month lull in which the rate of terrorist incidents had fallen to 100 a month, there was a sudden resurgence of violence. The incident rate rose to more than 400; and, although most of the raids were still aimed at securing support by terror, an increasing number were directed against the village police posts.

The policemen's lot was not a happy one. A typical Malayan rubber-tapping village might contain some 500 to 2,000 inhabitants —all Chinese. Even with the newly trained special constables, a village police station seldom had more than 10 or 12 men—all Malays. Although as Malays they were less likely to succumb to Communist subversion than if they had been Chinese, they could hardly feel confident of getting much help from the villagers if they were attacked by Chinese guerrillas. Moreover, in October, 1949, the Communist armies had overrun the mainland of China; and it seemed only a matter of time before they rolled on into Southeast Asia. Thus, few Malayan Chinese were willing to provide evidence of having actively helped the British–Malay Government fight the Communists.

Indeed, thanks to this factor and to the work of the newly strengthened Communist village organization, the raids on the police posts were usually supported from within the village. The police post would be surrounded, usually by a force of 100 or more, and the 10 or 12 policemen forced to surrender. Government officials would be murdered, especially if they were Chinese or if they were known to be unpopular, but the Malay policemen would more often be spared, after they had been disarmed and warned not to interfere in the future with the contacts between the people and the Liberation Army.

The Communists were undoubtedly wise to be lenient with the Malays. Had they murdered the policemen, they might have roused their friends and kinsmen in neighboring Malay kampongs from indifference to fury. Moreover, they knew that the British could replace dead policemen but that policemen who had been frightened might stay discreetly inside the police compound at night, leaving the Communists free to deal with "traitors" as they wished. The government would have the village marked with a reassuring blue pin on the map, but the Communists would control it.

A refinement of this tactic was for the Communist company commander to arrange a mock battle with the police post. After much shooting (with no casualties) the Communists would withdraw, having "captured" three or four rifles and a box of ammunition. The police sergeant (with the Chinese villagers corroborating) would describe how his heroic policemen had beaten off the raid, and he might earn a commendation for his gallantry.

Some of the police posts undoubtedly fell for this; but, to their credit, the great majority did not. Though their men were threatened, humiliated, offered bribes, and killed, the police force as a whole remained loyal. Where they did not, however, and made a live-and-let-live deal, that village became a Communist village, without any option, and every man, woman, and child in the village knew it. That was how the Communists usually started an oil spot, not by the spectacular capture of the village by armed guerrillas.

It was vital that we should have effective plans for the rapid reinforcement of village police posts under attack, plans in which the police themselves had confidence. From the start of the emergency, the main police district headquarters had standing orders to telephone the outlying posts every hour, and if there was no reply to act at once. Within four weeks, this procedure had proved itself; for on July 12, 1948, the Communists seized Batu Arang, Malaya's only coal mine, and overwhelmed the police post. The telephone line went dead, and at once a reinforcement squad set out from Rawang, eight miles away. The Communists, who had by this time sabotaged some of the mine's heavy machinery, did not wait to see how strong the reinforcements were; they withdrew at once.

This, we found, was quite normal; and indeed, it accords with Mao Tse-tung's doctrine: "When attacked, withdraw." In close country such as Malaya, it was hard for the guerrillas to assess what was behind a counterattack. All they knew was that well-trained, well-armed soldiers were advancing purposefully upon them; and so they pulled out. A quick, simple counterattack by a platoon would drive a raid off a village before it had gone too far, whereas a battalion attack two hours later would have found all the policemen dead and the guerrillas in full control.

As we gained experience, infantry battalions were spread out in company-sized camps, each company being responsible for patrolling the rubber estates and the neighboring jungle, and for aiding the village police posts in its area. These camps were not "forts" or "strong points"; they were merely living quarters for the soldiers. Their capture had no significance apart from the immediate loss of equipment, since the guerrillas could not hold them against counterattack; and indeed, apart from raids in search of weapons or ammunition, they seldom tried to attack them. Soldiers are usually the last targets chosen by guerrillas, unless they know that the troops' organization is weak and their morale low.

The camps were often empty except for a platoon resting after a long patrol; the others would be out in the rubber or the jungle.

It would be this platoon that rushed in armored trucks to help the police post under attack, in answer to a radio call, a Verey light signal, a telephone call, or simply a telephone line gone dead.

Why were these "brush-fire" platoons not more often ambushed? Because two or three armored wheeled vehicles are not easy to ambush (unlike the huge tracked armored columns used by the French in Indochina).[1] If they move fast and are well spread out, at least one vehicle will be outside the first blast of anything but a very complex ambush; and from this vehicle the soldiers will debouch unscathed and ready to cut off the ambush party. After a number of unpleasant experiences, the guerrillas in Malaya preferred to ambush "soft" vehicles.

Why, in spite of the vastly increased availability of helicopters, do the guerrillas in South Vietnam seem able to do what the Malayan Communists failed to do? The Viet Cong can attack villages in force, hold them for hours or even days in the face of strong airmobile counterattacks, and establish comprehensive positions that take a heavy toll of the counterattacking forces. My impression is that the South Vietnamese Army failed earlier to harass the Viet Cong sufficiently in their jungle bases, so that they have become practiced in living and operating in big formations; also, their communications are good enough to coordinate complex operations involving major attacks and multiple ambushes in battalion and regimental strength. By 1965, this had reached a situation beyond the power of the South Vietnamese Army to restore, and led to massive intervention of U.S. combat units. By escalating into the kind of war in which the U.S. can inevitably outbid them, the Viet Cong have probably signed their own death warrant. No one, however, would have wished for such escalation to occur, with all its casualties, destruction, and dangers, if the Viet Cong could have been held and defeated a few years back in a less expensive way.

In Malaya, although we made many mistakes in developing our tactics, we constantly harassed and raided the guerrillas in their jungle camps. They did not lose many men from these attacks, but they were kept on the move. Couriers failed to find them, messages failed to get through, and commanders found it impossible to co-

---

[1] For an account of the ambushing of French armored columns in Indochina, see Fall, *Street Without Joy*, chap. vii.

ordinate the operations of their regiments. At the same time, the Emergency Regulations (notably the curfews, travel restrictions, and checking of identity cards) made it difficult for the Communists to carry out coordination through their contacts in the villages, and certainly not tightly enough for complex military operations. This forced the Communist leaders to rely on the use of "quotas" for each regiment; they ordered the regiment during the coming month to ambush so many trains, kill so many government officials, destroy so many tin mines, slash so many rubber trees, and raid so many police posts. Thus, raids on police posts were generally isolated and bereft of coordinated support. Our reaction operations consequently were successful, and by and large, police morale endured.

This would not have been achieved, however, unless we had carried the war into the jungle, to harass and break up the big battalions.

As the thousands of new special constables completed their training early in 1949, more of the soldiers were becoming free to take the offensive; their task was to locate the big guerrilla camps, raid them, capture their weapons and food stocks, and eventually force them to split up into smaller gangs in order to survive.

Initially, because of their previous training and experience, senior army officers were inclined to launch their units into the jungle in battalion strength—either in giant encirclement operations when a camp was known to be in the area, or in wide sweeps based on no information at all. Neither of these types of operation had any success.

The predilection of some army officers for major operations seems incurable. Even in the late 1950's, new brigade commanders would arrive from England, nostalgic for World War II, or fresh from large-scale maneuvers in Germany. On arrival in Malaya, they would address themselves with grease pencils to a map almost wholly green except for one red pin. "Easy," they would say. "Battalion on the left, battalion on the right, battalion blocking the end, and then a fourth battalion to drive through. Can't miss, old boy." So a thousand long-suffering lieutenants, sergeants, and privates would be launched on an operation described by some name such as "hammer and anvil" or "splitting the disc" or "rabbit hunt."

These maneuvers are still described in U.S. Army textbooks,

though they were removed from the British ones long ago. Since it took the better part of a day, with more than a thousand soldiers, to get an effective cordon even a half-mile square around a jungle camp, the guerrillas, hearing the soldiers crashing through the jungle into position had no difficulty getting clear before the net was closed. Except for a rare brush with a straggler, all the soldiers ever found was an empty camp; but this enabled the officers to claim they had "cleared the area of enemy." This would be duly marked up on the maps, and the commanders would go to bed with a glow of satisfaction over a job well done. The soldiers, nursing their blisters, had other words for it.

Our best commanders in Malaya were the ones who set themselves the task of managing the war in such a way that their small patrols came face to face with the guerrillas on favorable terms; in other words, with good intelligence. This meant long hours of tactful discussions with police officers, administrators, rubber planters, tin miners, and local community leaders, getting them to cooperate with the soldiers and to promote the flow of information to them. Such commanders would regularly accompany their patrols, often placing themselves under the platoon commanders, so that they really understood the war and knew what was needed to win it.

In 1949, however, few commanders took this line; and thousands of soldiers spent thousands of hours "clearing the area of enemy" while the guerrillas continued to carry out their attacks on the police and the civil population.

Most of the kills in these early days were the result of purely chance contacts between the guerrillas and small army patrols that had been sent out for reconnaissance. Later, as the army gained experience, more and more of the kills were achieved by positive actions—for instance, by following tracks through the jungle and finding the camps, or by lying low and listening. In those days, with the Communists living in big camps of 100 men or more, the patrols often were able to hear voices, movements in the undergrowth, or the clatter of cooking pots long before they could see anything.

Some commanders, however, even after they learned that direct attacks were better than maneuvers, still clung to the notion that to attack a camp of 150 or 200 guerrillas, it was unsound to send a column .ess than 100 strong. In fact, as the junior officers themselves well knew, in a patrol raid (and still more in a chance contact) it is seldom possible in the jungle for anyone but the nearest 3 or 4 men on either side to see enough to shoot. They shoot just as well with 6 men behind them as they do with 96; and they have a far better chance of getting a shot because the enemy can hardly fail to hear the 96 tramping along, and will either get clear or be lying in concealed positions ready to ambush them.

The same appears to be true in South Vietnam, certainly in the jungle areas. An American adviser, reporting in 1963, wrote:

> In every instance where an envelopment of an objective through the jungle was planned, the column commander could not control or coordinate the enveloping forces. Even when two columns were only several kilometers apart, a four- or five-hour delay was encountered before the columns could get together. A coordinated attack in the jungle from anything but a column is extremely difficult. Generally, forming a skirmish line close to an objective will decrease the commander's control and cause sufficient noise to give away the attack.[2]

Malaya, 1949; Vietnam, 1963—we learned the same lessons. Guerrillas, whether operating in dozens or hundreds, do not sit still for four or five hours listening to soldiers crashing their way through the jungle all around them. Small patrols, preferably living in the same area of jungle for weeks on end, watching for tracks, lying low, and listening, have a far better chance of killing guerrillas.

In fact, the guerrillas seldom stood and fought for long when they were raided, even by a small fighting patrol; they knew that a modern army, particularly with helicopter support, could quickly rush more troops to the scene once the chips were down.

The best way to inflict casualties, therefore, was to locate the camp without being seen, deploy ambush parties on all the nearby jungle trails in spots well out of earshot of the camp (usually a mile or more away from it), and launch a small but determined assault. The guerrillas would then abandon the camp, escaping individually to a prearranged rendezvous not far away. From there, they would move *along the trails* to a new site. They used the trails

---

[2] Major Charles K. Nulsen, Jr., U.S. Army Adviser in Zone D (South Vietnam), letter, February, 1963.

because movement through virgin jungle was so slow and noisy that they would almost certainly be heard and caught, whereas they could lope along at three or four miles an hour on many of the trails. Thus, ambushes on these trails would pick off a few guerrillas every time, and this toll proved very effective in these days of the battles of the big battalions.

A clear picture of the development of infantry tactics in this period is found in an account of the life of a successful infantry battalion, *The Green Howards in Malaya—1949–52*, by Major J. B. Oldfield. This book tells about every kill or group of kills the battalion made. An analysis of these kills is revealing.

Their first four months of operations—September through December, 1949—coincided with the launching of the main Communist offensive. The guerrillas were still living and operating in groups of 100 or more, emerging from the jungle to create 15 or 20 incidents every day, and to kill 200 people—mainly policemen and civilians—every month. In this period, the battalion, toiling through the jungle, saw the guerrillas just five times, lost one man, and killed *one guerrilla*.

During the following six months (January–June, 1950), they killed a number of guerrillas by chance contacts; but they killed nearly twice as many by raiding camps they had located by tracking and listening. (They were also, incidentally, made to take part in at least two grandiose operations, each involving several battalions and lasting several weeks, in the course of which they killed no one at all.)

In their second year (1950–51), they more than doubled their kill-rate. But less than 25 per cent of their kills were now by chance contacts; 70 per cent were the result of tracking and listening, including a number by laying ambushes for the guerrillas they had located instead of raiding them.

# 7

# THE BRIGGS PLAN

By the spring of 1950, though we had survived two dangerous years, we were undoubtedly losing the war. The soldiers and police were killing guerrillas at a steady 50 or 60 a month and getting 20 or 30 surrenders, but the Communists were more than making up for this by good recruiting. The soldiers were killing about 6 guerrillas for every man they lost in the jungle, but the hard-pressed police posts were losing more men than the Communists. The guerrillas were murdering more than 100 civilians a month, and the police seemed powerless to prevent it. There was a growing danger that the police and the civilian population would lose confidence in the government and conclude that the guerrillas in the end must win.

The main reason why we were losing was that the guerrillas could get all the support they needed—food, clothing, information, and recruits—from the squatters. It was quite impossible to police or protect them. The squatter areas, in so far as they were governed at all, were ruled by the Communist parallel hierarchy, which the squatters accepted. Unlike their fellow Chinese in the villages, the squatters had little to lose from a collapse of the established order and economy; and besides, they had no option but to pay "taxes" and provide food for the guerrillas. Thus, the Communists were fast building up their strength and their support and at the same time stocking up arms and ammunition by raiding or corrupting the village police posts.

There was another problem. Nearly all the 200 policemen and civilians dying every month were in the rural areas. To avoid alarming the people, little publicity was given to these losses. News releases still spoke contemptuously of the gangs of "bandits" being "mopped up" in the jungle. As a result, large numbers of civil servants in the cities, and the bureaucratic elements of the police and military headquarters, were still working at a peacetime tempo; with little idea of the danger facing them, they indulged in petty jealousies and departmental feuds. There was, for example, friction between the old Malayan hands, who had endured Japanese captivity, and the new intake, who had a different outlook and very different manners. This was particularly so in the police, where large numbers of officers and sergeants had recently come from Palestine.[1] Fresh from a shooting war, these police officers thought they knew best; many got promotions. Even the new Commissioner of Police was from Palestine, and this was deeply resented by the men of the old regime. Finally, many of the police and civil servants were at odds with the brash young army officers who seemed to throw their weight around in a way that hardly befitted people who had been in the country only a few months. All this was childish and would have been swept away had there been an awareness of the gravity of the situation, but this the authorities had been at pains to conceal. With the situation still deteriorating after nearly two years, however, the British Government realized that a new approach was needed.

In April, 1950, therefore, the government appointed General Sir Harold Briggs as Director of Operations to act as the executive of the High Commissioner, Sir Henry Gurney. Briggs was given

---

[1] The British had in 1948 handed back their mandate in Palestine to the United Nations.

authority over all the security forces—army, police, and air force —and power to coordinate actions of civil departments that affected the war.

Briggs was a good man for the job. He had a fine record of jungle fighting in World War II and had spent most of his army life in Asia. He was imaginative and incisive, but also modest and tactful. Aged fifty-five, he had just retired from the army when he was asked by the government to take on this job. He agreed to do so for a year but actually stayed for 18 months, during which he devised and launched a plan for victory that not only won the war in Malaya but has been copied ever since in other countries facing similar emergencies.

The Briggs Plan is remembered chiefly for the resettlement of the 423,000 squatters into New Villages. This was certainly its biggest problem, but it looked far deeper than that. In his first directive, Briggs put his finger on what this war was really about— a competition in government. He aimed not only to resettle the squatters but to give them a standard of local government and a degree of prosperity that they would not wish to exchange for the barren austerity of life under the Communists' parallel hierarchy; in other words, to give them something to lose.

Militarily, as Briggs forecast two weeks after he arrived, this would create the vital ingredient for victory that was lacking: intelligence, the kind of precise intelligence that would bring the guerrillas to battle with the soldiers on the soldiers' ground.

Briggs also realized that his plan could never be effective unless there was better cooperation among the three arms of government —civil, police, and military—not only on the top level but right down into every district. To this end, he set up his office in Federal Police Headquarters and established a War Council[2] consisting of the Chief Secretary of the Federation, the Commissioner of Police, and the commanders of the army and the air force. Briggs himself presided, with the High Commissioner's authority. State War Executive Committees (SWEC's) were set up under the state prime ministers (or their executive secretaries) and in-

---

[2] Later, as the country approached Independence Day, the War Council evolved into an Emergency Operation Council (EOC), of which the Prime Minister was Chairman, the Defense Minister was Deputy Chairman, and the Director of Operations was Executive Officer.

cluded the states' chief police officers and army brigade commanders. Similarly, district officers with the district police officers
and army battalion commanders comprised the District War Executive Committees (DWEC's). The SWEC's and DWEC's thereafter
ran the war. (See Figure 2.)

FIGURE 2

STATE AND DISTRICT WAR EXECUTIVE COMMITTEES*

| SWEC | DWEC | RESPONSIBLE FOR: |
|---|---|---|
| *Civil* | | |
| State Prime Minister | District Officer | Local government |
| Executive Secretary | | Administration of Prime Minister's office |
| Information Officer | Information Officer | Public relations and psychological warfare |
| *Police* | | |
| Chief Police Officer | Police Commander | All police in district |
| Head, Special Branch | Special Branch Officer | Police intelligence |
| Military Intelligence Officer | Military Intelligence Officer | Assisting Special Branch |
| Home Guard Officer | Home Guard Officer | Training and administration of Home Guard |
| *Military* | | |
| Brigade Commander | Battalion Commander | All troops in district and requests for air support |

* Full meetings of the War Executive Committees were also attended by
unofficial members, such as community leaders and representatives of local
industries. These are not shown in Figure 2.

In all these committees, the chairman was the civilian administrator—the state prime minister or the district officer. This
was because he was responsible for law and order, and the aim of
all operations was to restore his area to a condition in which he
could govern without the army and with only normal police support.
Also, the major factor in deciding when it was wise to lift restrictions and dispense with soldiers was the attitude of the people, and

the civil administrator was the best man to judge when military operations might hinder rather than help to win their support.

The police and military members were the commanders in person, not staff officers. This meant they could make decisions on their own instead of having to say, "I will ask the brigadier if he can do it."

In addition to these three full members, there were a number of other officials always in attendance, notably the police Special Branch officer, the state or district information officer (who also handled psychological warfare), the Home Guard officer, and a food control officer.

The Home Guard units operated under the command of the district police, not of the Home Guard officer, who was responsible only for their recruiting, training, and administration, and who attended the War Executive Committee only in an advisory capacity.

The Special Branch officer was not a full member either, since he was the subordinate of the state or district police officer.[3] He was, however, always present, and was assisted by a military intelligence officer (MIO), whose function was to collate, interpret, and present intelligence in such a way that it could be exploited by army patrols and ambushes. He was responsible to the Special Branch, not to the army. When, for example, an intelligence project was in too delicate a stage to exploit, the MIO could not release it to the army without Special Branch permission. This was sometimes a point of irritation to enthusiastic army officers, but it was very necessary.

A later development was the inclusion of unofficial members in SWEC's and DWEC's. These were community leaders, selected by the chairman of the SWEC or DWEC, to represent the major local industries and the main racial and religious groups. Thus, among the official and unofficial members there would always be at least one Malay, one Indian, and one Chinese. The inclusion of these unofficial members proved a great success. They could, for example,

---

[3] The police commander on a large District War Executive Committee was usually in fact the OSPC (officer superintending police circle) with his "circle" Special Branch officer. The "circle" was a police level in between state and district designed to spread the responsibility, but for simplicity the term "district" is used to incorporate both police circle and district staff in this book.

advise if an adjustment of the curfew or the opening of a closed route would improve public support by enabling the people to increase their earnings. Moreover, since they shared the general desire to see an end of guerrilla warfare, they were able to explain to their own people why this or that restriction was necessary to achieve this end.

There were, of course, many Jeremiahs who forecast terrible security leaks through the unofficial members to the Communists; but the risk was amply justified, and the participation of the unofficial members in making SWEC and DWEC decisions was a major psychological factor in the acceptance by the people of the restrictions they were asked to endure.

The full SWEC and DWEC usually met only once a week to make plans and discuss problems. But an operations subcommittee met for about half an hour every morning. These daily sessions were known as "morning prayers."

Morning prayers were attended by five or six people at most —normally the basic triumvirate of civil, police, and military commanders, plus the Special Branch man and his MIO. Proceedings would start with a briefing by the MIO on the events of the past twenty-four hours. The commanders would decide whether to modify operations in progress or whether to prepare to exploit some opportunity, perhaps arising from information from a newly surrendered guerrilla or from documents captured in the night. The presence of the brigade or battalion commander would enable these chances to be seized in time; for example, a decision to concentrate two companies to cordon and search a village could be implemented within an hour or two of morning prayers. Moreover, this daily meeting ensured that sources of friction were nipped in the bud, and it became a matter of pride for the DWEC triumvirate to resolve their disagreements without whining to their respective superiors on the SWEC.

The first task that fell to these committees demanded the concentrated efforts of the district officers and of the bulk of the police and soldiers. This was the resettlement of the 423,000 squatters, which was accomplished in one year. Inevitably, there were errors and injustices. The problems, however, were solved in the end; and the most striking justification of the plan and its execution is that to this day virtually none of the people have moved again.

Although for five years they have been free to live where they please, they have preferred to stay on[4] in the villages to which they were moved—often against their will and sometimes by force— in 1950–51.

Some were moved into extensions of existing villages, but the majority were resettled in about 400 New Villages. The selection of sites for these New Villages involved many factors. They had to be defensible and not too close to the jungle fringe, but near where the people would work. They had to have access to roads and water. The ground had to be flat enough to build on but not subject to flooding in one of the wettest climates in the world. (Most such ground, of course, was already in use; and thousands of acres of cultivated land had to be requisitioned.) The space was based on an 800-square-yard patch for each family, enough to raise a few chickens and grow vegetables, within the defended perimeter; in addition, each family that grew its own food was allowed two acres of arable land within two miles of the village. These plots were not fenced off and were guarded only when the crops were ripe enough to eat.

Once the surveys had been made, the land was cleared, the water supply and drainage installed, and a barbed-wire fence[5] erected around the village—either to keep the people in or the guerrillas out, depending on who was describing it. Timber frames were erected for the houses, with roofs of atap (palm leaves) or corrugated iron. The walls were to be added by the new occupants, with materials provided. The settlers also were given a grant on which to live while they moved in.

The roundup and movement of the squatters had to be conducted as an operation of war, partly because they had been warned by the Communists not to cooperate and partly because they were frightened of what it all meant. As squatters, although they had to pay levies to the Communists, they could at least be certain of growing enough food to keep alive, and they were loath to give up their land.

---

[4] Kernial Singh, "The Saga of the Malayan Squatter," *Journal of South East Asian History*, V, No. 1 (March, 1964), 169.

[5] Barbed wire was later often replaced by a chain-link fence, which was a much better obstacle and made the villages seem less like "concentration camps," as Communist propaganda described them.

When the skeleton of a New Village was ready, a selected squatter area would be surrounded before dawn by a cordon of troops. Other troops, police, nurses, and welfare officers moved into the area. Each family was allowed to fill one truck with its possessions, food, and a limited amount of livestock. The families were repaid at market prices for any animals or crops that could not be taken along.

In the long run, these early-morning roundups were among the most important moments of the war, for the way they were conducted colored the whole attitude of the people toward the government. The roundups could have been carried out with brutality, as Communist propaganda had led the squatters to expect. In fact, however, they were carried out with much kindness and sympathy. For the British soldiers could not fail to feel sorry for these bewildered families, being torn from their homes and livelihood without warning, sitting miserably with a pathetic bundle of possessions, waiting for the truck to take them away. The Chinese stick together as families, and there would be old women, young children, and babies. For the soldiers it was a hateful task, and there was nothing false about the compassion with which they helped these families gather up the chickens, carry the babies, and lift the old women into the trucks. This astonished the Chinese, and many have since placed on record that it was one of the biggest factors in winning their eventual support.

Because the squatters were not accustomed to community life, administration in the New Villages was a problem requiring tact and understanding. Each New Village was set up by a Chinese-speaking British resettlement officer with the assistance of one or two young Malayan Chinese, who took over the administration when the British official moved on to start the next village. Finding 200 British officers for this temporary duty was not easy; though many officials spoke Malay, few spoke Chinese dialects. Briggs, however, insisted that all government departments release their most able Chinese-speaking officials for these jobs. Other persons were brought in from outside, including missionaries who had been ousted from China by Mao Tse-tung. In addition, 400 Malayan Chinese, willing to live in the villages and face the constant threat of assassination by the Communists, also had to be found.

All the officers had to be selected carefully, for the jobs offered exceptional opportunities for graft. An unscrupulous official could take bribes from families for special favors or conduct lucrative rackets with merchants who provided building materials. Legislation to prevent this was inserted in the Emergency Regulations, and the rare offenders were severely punished when caught. The great majority of resettlement officers, however—particularly the Chinese —did a dangerous and frustrating job with courage, integrity, and skill.

By the middle of 1951, most of the resettlement was completed. The Communists, disappointed once again by the lack of revolutionary self-sacrifice among the masses, reacted with violence, the only weapon they had left. Incidents and casualties reached their peak. The "disloyal" villages were raked with machine-gun fire from the jungle-covered hills; night raiders penetrated the village fences to murder collaborators, resettlement officers, and village policemen. The government army, still short of specific intelligence, slogged through the jungle, killing more guerrillas than before but still not enough to offset their growing strength from new recruits.

In October, 1951, the guerrillas achieved their greatest triumph. They ambushed and killed the High Commissioner himself, Sir Henry Gurney, in spite of a powerful army escort on the road. For the British and the loyal Malayans, this was the darkest moment of the insurgency.

But the enemy, too, was having grave difficulties. Faced with the fact that the guerrillas were not winning the support of the people by intimidation, the Central Committee issued a directive just before the October ambush ordering that, while attacks on government officials, police posts, and active collaborators would continue, the guerrillas were under no circumstances to attack innocent people, either at work or in the villages.

Furthermore, the guerrillas were concerned about their own casualties. Although things seemed to be going their way, their losses in 1951 were double those of 1950 because the infantry was learning how to locate their big camps in the jungle. To survive, they would need to operate in smaller groups that could move quietly without leaving tracks, yet still carry out the new policy. They therefore ordered their regiments and companies to split up into platoons, which would conduct selective "hit-and-run" raids instead of wholesale terror and destruction.

The government had won a major victory, though this was not to become apparent until the middle of the following year. For three and one-half years the police posts had been under the threat of attack by companies of 200 guerrillas; under the new Communist directive, these attacks were to be staged by units of only 20 or 30 men, against whom the police posts could hold out until help came. The direct result was that monthly police losses were to plunge from 100 in 1951 to 20 by the middle of 1952 and were never to rise above that figure again. Similarly, in 1951, 90 civilians had been killed every month; but by mid-1952, the figure was 15 —also never to rise again. These were the dividends of population control and of breaking up the big battalions.

Neither of the authors of this victory lived to realize what they had achieved. When the guerrillas killed Sir Henry Gurney, he knew nothing of the new directive they had been forced by his efforts to issue to their units. And when Gurney died, Sir Harold Briggs already was in the process of handing over his duties to his deputy, Sir Rob Lockhart. Worn out by his efforts, Briggs died a few months later without knowing that the tide had turned.

# 8

## MALAYA AND VIETNAM— THE CRITICAL YEARS

T HE insurgency in South Vietnam reached a crisis at the end of 1963 in many ways parallel to the crisis in Malaya at the end of 1951. In both cases, the war took a new turn, in Malaya for the better and in South Vietnam for the worse. In both cases, a large-scale resettlement of the population had been completed and a positive plan of campaign had been devised. In Malaya, the government thereafter grew in strength to independent viability; in South Vietnam, the government dissolved into a prolonged period of instability. In Malaya, the next two years saw a steady decline in the size of guerrilla units and the scale of their violence; in South Vietnam, these escalated faster than ever before, leading to massive reinforcement from North Vietnam on one side and from the United States on the other.

It is tempting for Western analysts to look for consolation by ascribing this escalation solely to reinforcement across the border from North Vietnam. Though this was an important factor, it is dangerous to allow it to conceal the other factors. Viet Cong rein-forcements from North Vietnam would have been ineffective and easily destroyed if they had not had a popular base to support them; indeed, according to Mao Tse-tung's principle that guerrilla fish can survive only in a friendly sea, they would probably never have been sent. Nor does the *total number* of guerrillas in the country dictate the *size of units* in which they can operate. Even at the peak of guerrilla strength in Malaya, one government patrol spent weeks in the jungle for every contact. These patrols could have operated just as freely and far more profitably against twice as many guerrillas; they would have had twice as many contacts and probably would have suffered and inflicted twice as many casualties. Our casualty rate still would have been well within bearable bounds, but the guerrillas still would have been forced to operate in smaller units. And, as we saw in Chapter 6, it was the *size* of the guerrilla units, not their profusion, that decided the via-bility of the police and of the thread of local government in the villages.

There were many differences in the social and occupational en-vironments in Malaya and Vietnam. For example, Malaya in 1951 was still under a form of colonial government, and the guerrillas and their supporters were not of the same race as the bulk of the soldiers and police.[1] These differences, however, do not mean that this phase of the war in South Vietnam need necessarily have been lost. I believe that the story of the critical years in Malaya (1948–51) gives some important clues as to why it was lost—and perhaps even of how the war may eventually be won. In Malaya, population control was enforced by an effective local government; intimidation was kept in check by viable village police posts, whose integrity was maintained by the operations of the army. These things were not achieved in the parallel years in South Vietnam (1957–63). Despite the conditions, I believe that they could have been done,

---

[1] It is sometimes wrongly supposed that in Malaya the "guerrillas were, for the most part, physically distinguishable from the peaceful majority they sought to control" (Department of State Paper 7839, February, 1965, p. 1). In fact, the war was fought by Chinese guerrillas among almost wholly Chinese squatters and villagers, control of whom would have given them control of the economy of the country. The only people in the Chinese villages who were physically distinguishable from the guerrillas were the handful of uniformed Malay policemen.

that the war would not have escalated if they had been done, and that eventually they must be done if any victory, however it may be won, is to be permanent.

In both campaigns, an attempt was made to resettle the vulnerable part of the population into defensible villages. The gigantic Strategic-Hamlet Program was initiated in South Vietnam in April, 1962, aided by a British advisory mission led by the former Secretary for Defense in Malaya, R. K. G. (now Sir Robert) Thompson. Within two years, 12,000 Strategic Hamlets were to be established,[2] compared with 400 New Villages in one and one-half years in Malaya.

Apart from the scale of it, resettlement in Vietnam was a far more difficult problem than it had been in Malaya. The Malayan Chinese squatters had few real roots in the land; even if deprived of their small holdings, they could earn money in the rubber estates and tin mines. We were lucky that in 1951–52 the Korean War had caused a boom demand for rubber, and the resettled squatters had good opportunities for employment with high wages; so long as they could earn enough money, they did not care much where they lived. Many Vietnamese farmers tilled their own land and did care —a lot.

The terrain in Vietnam also makes resettlement more difficult, particularly in the Mekong Delta, where often the only unflooded land for houses is along the built-up flood banks of the rivers and canals. A strip of houses ten miles long and ten yards wide is far harder to defend than any of the villages we had in Malaya.

The Strategic-Hamlet Program, once begun, was forced through with tremendous urgency. Province chiefs were ordered to establish a given number of hamlets by a given date; and this they did, often failing to provide the people with adequate alternative means of earning money and leaving them in locations so far from their work and markets that transportation costs were prohibitive.[3] The inhabitants of the hamlets were not properly registered; nor were they policed against terror within or guarded against attack from outside.

Registration and the issuance of identity cards were attempted

---

[2] Fall, *The Two Viet-Nams*, p. 373.
[3] *Ibid.*, chap. xvi.

in parts of Vietnam, but failed. As one U.S. adviser saw it, "VC agents roam almost every place at will. If we use ID cards they catch the people in the field and make them tear them up, and if they feel like it they will report it—if not, they don't. Why should they? No one ever checks them."[4] This lack of effective registration gave the Viet Cong several important advantages not enjoyed by the Communists in Malaya. First, their guerrillas or agents, regular or part-time, could move into a village and live among the people without any serious risk of being picked up in a police check. Second, in the fields, the guerrillas could hide their weapons and mingle with the workers on the approach of government forces, who then had no means of detecting the guerrillas unless some worker was brave enough to denounce them. Third, Viet Cong couriers could and did move freely in public transport.

The people, in fact, suffered all the disadvantages of resettlement with none of the advantages, either in terms of social amenities or of security. With little to stop them but a perimeter fence patrolled by part-time armed villagers and with their own agents already inside, the Viet Cong were able to overrun large numbers of these hamlets; and this had a disastrous effect on public confidence.

The Strategic-Hamlet Program in 1962–63 failed to achieve its goal, not because it was in itself wrong but because it was not accompanied by adequate defense, adequate regulations for population control, or adequate local government and police forces within the hamlets. Resettlement is like the roof of a house, and these other measures are like the walls. A roof cannot keep out the cold if the walls are full of holes, but this does not mean the roof is not good.[5]

---

[4] Major Robert B. Osborn, U.S. Army, letter from Vietnam, February 18, 1965.

[5] Milton E. Osborne, in an interesting comparison between resettlement in Malaya and Vietnam, writes:

One is still left with the conclusion that some form of rural control had to be established by the Saigon Government. That the strategic hamlet program did not approach the achievement of this goal was closely linked with Nhu's insistence on quantity rather than quality in hamlet construction and development. But the time for the establishment of a careful program of rural control and development was at least seven years ago.

In *Strategic Hamlets in South Viet-Nam—A Survey and a Comparison*, pp. 56–57.

The local government in South Vietnam, at district and village level, has seldom been able to enforce even those regulations for population control that were introduced; it certainly would not have been able to enforce the much more comprehensive Emergency Regulations used in Malaya. One reason often advanced for this is that during the critical years in Malaya there was British supervision. In fact, there were no British officials at all in the villages (other than the district capitals), except for the temporary resettlement officers who stayed on for the first few months after the establishment of each New Village. Though British supervision and experience undoubtedly helped, the administration on the ground, where it mattered most, was by Malayans.

A second and more valid reason often cited is that the Malayan officials had a stronger motivation than the Vietnamese. Most of them were Malays, to whom a Communist victory meant a Chinese takeover; the other officials (Indians and Chinese), generally recruited from families with a commercial background, also would have had much more to lose under Communism. This cut both ways, however, in that both the Malays and Chinese *towkay* (merchant) classes were somewhat out of sympathy with the Chinese laborers in the villages, many of whom had both social and racial reasons to hope for a Chinese Communist victory. There is no doubt, in fact, that popular support for Communism in the New Villages was initially far stronger than it ever was among the South Vietnamese peasants.

Motivation of the village officials is, all the same, one of the key factors. This was often achieved at province level in South Vietnam, where regular army officers were appointed province chiefs. They were not only more competent than the usual middle-level civil servants, but they also had a personal stake in victory; as career officers who had volunteered for government service, they knew that they would get short shrift from a victorious Viet Cong regime. Although there are grave risks in military control of civil posts, these appointments undoubtedly proved worth while.

At the lower levels, some of the district and village chiefs were understandably less willing to take responsibility and enforce unpopular measures. They knew that if the Viet Cong took over, their only hope of survival would be to establish a claim that they did no more than they were forced to do by the "oppressive" government and its soldiers.[6] A more stark and compelling reason, however, has been the ever-present threat by Viet Cong agents living in the villages to kill the officials and their families. This threat, in fact, faced Malayan government officials in the early stages of the war. The number of civilians killed in Malaya in the three years 1948–50 (500, 700, 1,200) was on a similar scale to that in South Vietnam in 1957–59 (700, 1,200, and 2,500), bearing in mind that South Vietnam has double Malaya's population. In Malaya, these killings were down in 1951 to 1,000; but in 1960 in South Vietnam, they soared to 4,000 and have gone on rising, sometimes reaching more than 100 a day. Once this kind of terror begins to get out of hand, it becomes progressively harder to restore confidence and reverse the trend. The question is whether in Vietnam it need ever have got out of hand, or whether it would have been possible to create an effective police force to check it in 1957–59. Whether or not it is relevant today, a detailed study of that question might yield big dividends in future insurgencies.

This brings us back to the decisive character in this drama, the village policeman. The police in South Vietnam in 1963 were still in the same stages as in Malaya, in June, 1948, able to deal only with normal peacetime civil and criminal offenses, not with wholesale murder and terror sponsored by an organized political party. In Malaya, we expanded our police force sevenfold; but in South Vietnam, the task has been left to the army and the paramilitary Popular Force.

A friend commenting on these views from Vietnam in July, 1965, wrote:

> The real root of the problem unfortunately *does* lie in whether people can or cannot sleep in reasonable security at night inside the villages. They cannot, in fact, sleep with any security at all. They are insecure because there are no policemen because no one wants to be a police-

---

[6] In a conversation, Sir Robert Thompson described a vivid example of this:

The Viet Cong occupied a village in which the village chief had been cooperating with the government. They assembled the villagers, and forced them and the village chief to watch while they disemboweled his wife before his eyes. They then cut off the arms and legs of his children, one by one. Finally they emasculated the village chief himself. No one else in the village was touched.

man. No one wants to be a policeman because the VC will kill any-one who arrests or interferes with them.

A well-armed, well-trained and sufficiently large force of village police would have been an invaluable tool against the VC when they were small bandit groups. . . . In cooperation with some form of properly armed mobile force, such a force might well have controlled the VC from the beginning. The PF . . . are absolutely not an effective substitute for regular police, and regular police are not found in the hamlet.[7]

There is a very real difference between a trained policeman and a part-time villager in the Popular Forces or, as we called them in Malaya, the Home Guard. We had five or six home guardsmen for every constable in Malaya; and while only one in seven was on duty at a time, the others could be called out in emergency to fight against raids on the village. Their task, however, was to assist in the defense of the village from outside. Walking the streets to deter and detect the terrorist murders of civilians in their beds was the task of the police, who were backed by an intelligence system and were trained to deal with terror as an extension of criminal gang warfare. By 1949, they had sufficient strength to take up this task; by 1951, they had begun to master it.

The emergency training of armed villagers usually takes only a week or two, with periodic refreshers, and is largely confined to shooting and squad tactics. A police constable's training takes six months and covers a wide field of law enforcement and detection. The police recruit should not be a "local boy" from the village—certainly not under insurgency conditions, where the emotional and coercive pressures on him would be a serious disadvantage. If the internal security of Chinese New Villages had been left entirely in the hands of the Chinese Home Guard, the war in Malaya probably would have gone the same way as in Vietnam.

As well as selection and training, constables need motivation and supervision. Except for the handpicked Chinese Special Branch detectives, the village constables were Malays, their noncommissioned officers were regular Malay policemen with some experience, and their commanders at the district level included a number of long-service British police officers.

---

[7] Major Osborn, letter from Vietnam, July 13, 1965.

Some of my friends who have served in Vietnam doubt whether it would have been possible to form a village police force capable of preventing the free movement of Viet Cong agents inside the villages and deterring terrorism. These friends suggest that men of the necessary character and motivation were not available in sufficient numbers, that in any case their motivation would not have survived the immediate intimidation or the long-term lack of confidence in victory, and that these shortcomings applied even more to the supervisory grades. Concluding that terror in Vietnam can only be deterred by military retaliation, they suggest that the best men must be recruited into the army.

This, however, is not a majority view, and I believe that it is wrong. Indeed, to say that it is impossible to devise any means of maintaining law and order short of calling in the army is to admit that free government will not work in Vietnam.

The number of trained policemen required is large but not prohibitive. In Malaya, we raised the number from 9,000 to 45,000 in six months; eventually it passed 60,000. Based on this experience, it would seem that to provide adequate police posts in South Vietnamese villages, about 100,000 men, backed by the existing Popular Forces and by the army, might be needed.[8] These 100,000 would inevitably be a direct drain on recruitment for the army. In this kind of war, however, the internal security of inhabited areas must have priority over defense against outside attack—for which it is, in any case, a prerequisite. Foreign troops (Americans, Australians, South Koreans) can relieve the army in the jungle, but the village policemen *must* be Vietnamese.

Do 100,000 suitable recruits exist? Some could be found in the

---

[8] Majòr Obsorn, writing from Vietnam in July, 1965, told me that he had recommended officially:

There should be at least one well-trained National Policeman for every 200 people in every hamlet. There should be at least one platoon plus one squad of Popular Force in every hamlet of 1,000–1,500 inhabitants, and there should be two Regional Force companies not in static positions in each District. As long as the people are not protected from without and within there can be no effective Rural Reconstruction.

On this basis, 9 million rural inhabitants would require 45,000 national policemen. Even allowing for the many other calls for police, my estimate of 100,000 is a generous one.

army ranks, others among the South Vietnamese farm families, who have no desire to be collectivized. From these two sources, there surely must be men available with the proper character and motivation.

Though policemen are more vital than soldiers, police posts cannot function if they are under constant threat from guerrilla units many times their size. The army in Malaya prevented this by harassing the big guerrilla units until they were forced to split up and by disrupting their communications so that they could not coordinate or concentrate their units.

I see three main causes for the failure to prevent it in South Vietnam: Ineffective registration and control of the population have allowed Viet Cong commanders and units to keep in touch freely through public channels; commanders have been reluctant to send small numbers of soldiers against large guerrilla units; and massive airmobile operations against big Viet Cong units have left few men available for harassment patrols.

It has been suggested that South Vietnamese soldiers are temperamentally unsuited for small-scale raids against large enemy units. This cannot be true; they are of the same stock as the Viet Cong, and many proved their worth with the Viet Minh in similar raids against the French. If they have failed, it must be from lack of motivation and leadership.

Massed helicopter operations are certainly effective in open terrain; this was proved in Algeria as well as in Vietnam. But 80 per cent of South Vietnam is covered by jungle, rubber trees, or swamp, making it easy for the Viet Cong to evade or ambush airmobile assaults. As Bernard Fall wrote at the end of 1963, "it is clear that there is still no panacea in the field of counterguerrilla operations when one has to commit 5,000 men for three days, with all the paraphernalia of a D-Day landing, to come out with a dead count of 9 out of perhaps 500 enemy troops under attack."[9] Even though a number of these large-scale operations have no doubt succeeded, the helicopters should have been better used in smaller numbers to help local officials visit their villages more often, to react to raids quickly and sharply rather than with giant encirclements hours

---

[9] Fall, *The Two Viet-Nams*, p. 381.

later, and to saturate chosen areas quickly with numerous small patrols. These would have been better ways to break the big Viet Cong units down to a manageable size.

The physical intervention across the borders of South Vietnam has now assumed gigantic proportions. This, however, is a relatively recent development, as was brought out in State Department Publication No. 7839 of February, 1965. Before 1964, most of the infiltrators along the Ho Chi Minh Trail were South Vietnamese returning after training in the North. In 1964, there was a marked increase in infiltrators, 90 per cent of whom were reported to be of North Vietnamese stock; they brought with them an increasing number of Russian and Chinese weapons.

Through the critical years, however, to the end of 1963, it was largely a South Vietnamese war, fought by South Vietnamese guerrillas, supplied by South Vietnamese villagers, and armed with weapons captured from French or South Vietnamese soldiers. This was confirmed in March, 1963, by a senior U.S. general in Vietnam.[10] North Vietnam was a sanctuary from which the Hanoi government could direct the Viet Cong, to which guerrillas and cadres could be withdrawn for training, and in which regular units could be held in readiness for the eventual escalation of the war. The material effect of the border on the guerrilla fighting itself in these years was much exaggerated, often used as an alibi for failures that had quite different causes.[11] It also induced the government to give priority to frontier defense rather than to internal danger in training and organizing its army.

The 1963 political crisis—the Buddhist uprisings and other unrest that brought the overthrow of the Diem government—led the Communists to believe that the time was ripe for escalation into "mobile" or "conventional" war. This was answered by retaliation against North Vietnam, the sanctuary from which the escalation was being launched. Whether this forces the Viet Cong back to guerrilla warfare or leads to an acceptable political settlement, the weaknesses that produced the 1963 crisis will eventually have to be put right. Even a Korean-type victory would achieve nothing

---

[10] *The Washington Post,* March 6, 1963.

[11] "To lay stress on the number of men who have infiltrated from the North is to avoid recognition of the response which they have achieved in the South." Osborne, *op. cit.,* p. 56.

unless it resulted in the declared aim of the "establishment of the authority of the Government in Saigon over all the territory South of the 17th parallel."[12] Indeed, what else could be the aim of this or any other military operation? Once established, no local administration will survive the inevitable Communist efforts to dislodge or subvert it unless there is efficient population control by a viable local police force with proper support from the army.

Amid the thunder of the bombing and the major operations, very hopeful signs have appeared in South Vietnam, in terms of stability, security, and morale. It was good to hear from a friend in April, 1965, that there had been:

> another major breakthrough in our province in the last few days— we now have a civilian province chief, with the provincial committee system. We now have our morning meetings and are beginning to get all factions together and present some sort of united front. This may sound like nought to you, but it calls for rejoicing as far as we are concerned.[13]

The New-Life Hamlet Program is taking a much more sober approach to resettlement than the attempt to string fences around 12,000 Strategic Hamlets in 1962-63. It has begun with a realistic plan to pacify 300 hamlets. This incorporates a painstaking intelligence operation to identify Viet Cong agents and sympathizers, establishment of local government with protection that can be sustained, and tangible social improvements, particularly in health and medical care.

Military tactics are being geared to the task of harassing the Viet Cong so that they are unable to operate with enough strength to overwhelm the Popular Force defenses of the pacified hamlets. As an example, the U.S. adviser in a paddy-growing district near Saigon gave this report of the activities of the Regional and Popular Forces, which are now under single direction:

> These troops establish ambushes each night and conduct small (two- or three-platoon) operations virtually every day. Thus the entire district is covered once every two or three weeks and, in consequence,

---

[12] State Department Publication No. 7724, August, 1964, p. 5.
[13] Major Osborn, letter from Quang Ngai Province, South Vietnam, April 3, 1965.

there are no permanent Vietcong bases within our limits. VC activity is confined to indigenous guerrillas and raids, typically of squad size by units based near the district's borders. Roads are in general not safe at night; during daylight one can with a small bodyguard enjoy freedom of the district.[14]

This accords precisely with our experience in Malaya. If it leads to better security and better intelligence, pacification will mean something. This kind of thoroughness, of course, makes progress slow, but this is far better than discrediting the whole idea by rushing into another series of failures. The patience and power of the U.S. have given the South Vietnamese Government a second chance; but this chance, too, will be thrown away unless the foundations are laid for stable and effective government in the villages, both to win the war and to maintain the peace.[15]

---

[14] The writer of this report in February, 1965, is not known. It was quoted to me by another U.S. Army adviser in Vietnam.

[15] For an excellent report of the progress made in this little publicized program of pacification, see Charles Mohr, "To Win People to Win the War," *The New York Times,* February 13, 1966, sec. E, p. 4. Mohr draws attention to the modest but realistic target of pacifying about 10 per cent of the population in 1966.

TWO

OFFENSIVE (1952-55)

# 9

## SIR GERALD TEMPLER

IF neither Gurney nor Briggs realized that the tide was turning in Malaya in October, 1951, the government and the people realized it even less. There was an intense atmosphere of crisis, and this was just what the country needed. If the High Commissioner himself could not be protected, who was safe? His assassination sent a wave of shock through the country, jolting the people in the cities out of their apathy.

Paradoxically, too, the very audacity of the ambush had a sobering effect on the Chinese in the New Villages. They knew that drastic reaction was inevitable, indeed, anything other than drastic action would only have earned contempt. They braced themselves for the wrath to come, taking more care not to bring it down on their own families by being seen to have Communist sympathies.

The British Government, too, was shaken. With both Gurney and Briggs gone, the government decided to combine the posts of

High Commissioner and Director of Operations and to give the new appointee overriding powers in every aspect of the government of the country. The man selected for this temporary dictatorship was General Sir Gerald Templer.

Templer was a surprise choice. Pale, wiry, and intense, he did not fit the popular idea of a military strong man. But he had the brain, the character, and the experience for the job. Twice decorated for fighting guerrillas in Palestine in 1936, wounded as a divisional commander in 1944, he ran the military government of the British zone of Germany in 1945. Subsequently, as head of intelligence and then of operations in the War Office in London, he was intimately concerned with the early stages of the Malayan insurgency. He came to Malaya knowing exactly what he wanted to do.

The dictatorship lasted only as long as proved necessary—two years. In that period, two-thirds of the guerrillas were wiped out, the terrorist incident rate fell from 500 a month to less than 100, and the casualty rate went from 200 to less than 40.

The process, of course, had already begun. Templer made no major changes in the plan, for he sensed that it was going well. He was the middle stage of a three-stage rocket. He could not have functioned without the first stage (Briggs); nor would the nation have reached its present orbit without the third stage, of which Tunku Abdul Rahman was the leader. The first stage was the toughest; the third was the longest, requiring the greatest finesse; the second was the most dynamic, and Templer was a most dynamic man.

The British Government's directive appointing Sir Gerald as High Commissioner and Supreme Commander of all land, sea and air forces, began: "The policy of the British Government is that Malaya should in due course become a fully self-governing nation." It may not be carrying the analogy too far to say that, unless the third stage and the final orbit are planned and maintained as the aim, the first and second stages are a waste of effort.

Templer from the start insisted that the fighting of the war and the civil running of the country were "completely and utterly interrelated." The destruction of the insurgency was merely part of the process of bringing the new country to independence. The aim was the creation of a way of life, "not necessarily the British way, nor the American way; it must be the Malayan way of life."

Templer was, however, impatient with the idea of "independence before breakfast." He realized that, for the people in the villages, self-government was less important than good government. He was determined to bring self-government to Malaya, but not until the independent government could be strong enough to prevent racial violence (as had occurred in India) and the people were no longer in a state of insecurity and poverty. The tragedy of the Congo has since proved how right he was.[1]

Within a few weeks of Templer's arrival, there was an incident that had a profound influence on the war.

Fifty miles north of Kuala Lumpur was the district capital of Tanjong Malim, a rubber-tapping town with a population of 20,000, mainly Chinese. The town received its water supply from a reservoir two miles up in the hills, and the pipeline from this reservoir had been cut five times by No. 36 Platoon of the Malayan Races' Liberation Army. In March, 1952 (presumably not yet having received Chin Peng's new directive), the guerrillas cut it again. For the sixth time, the town was without water; and for the sixth time, the repair party went out, this time with a police escort and the assistant district officer, a young and popular war hero named Michael Codner. Born in Malaya, Codner was recognized even by the enemy as a devoted and efficient administrator who served his people well. The guerrillas ambushed the repair party, killing or wounding all but one member. Codner was among the dead.

The people of the town were shocked by the incident, but they were also terrified of the Communists. Police questioning produced no information.

Three days later, Templer himself descended on Tanjong Malim. He assembled 300 of the leading citizens in the local auditorium. He spoke to them in a quiet fury, reminding them that in the last three months the guerrillas around their town had killed 15 people, attacked the railway twice, ambushed the road 10 times, burned

---

[1] As Richard Lawson wrote about the Congo in his book *Strange Soldiering*: "Independence may be a joy to the overfed politician in the capital, but to the man in the bush it means murder, pillage and rape. If he is lucky it means none of these things, but merely poverty and loneliness."

8 trucks and buses, and destroyed 6,000 rubber trees. The people who suffered from these attacks were the people of Tanjong Malim, yet the guerrillas were getting food from the town and could not have carried out most of these raids without help and information from the people. On the other hand, on only three occasions had anyone tried to help the police. Now the guerrillas had cut off the town's water supply and had killed 12 of the men going out to repair it.

"This," he said, "is going to stop. It does not amuse me to punish innocent people, but many of you are not innocent. You have information which you are too cowardly to give."[2]

He invoked the Emergency Regulation that empowered him to impose collective punishment. Tanjong Malim would forthwith cease to be the district capital, and the local government would be shifted to another town. To prevent them from contacting the guerrillas, the people would be confined to their houses for twenty-two hours of the day, being allowed out only for two hours while the shops were open. Their ration of rice, already kept down to reasonable daily needs, was cut in half. These restrictions would be maintained until the people proved they were ready to co-operate in ridding their district of terrorism.

He then announced that every family would be given a sheet of paper on which to write anything they knew about the guerrillas or about people they suspected of supporting them. These papers were delivered by soldiers and policemen, who called again twenty-four hours later with sealed boxes into which the papers, folded and unsigned, were placed. The boxes were then accompanied to Kuala Lumpur by community leaders, who watched Templer open them, keeping his promise that no one but himself would see the papers and that, when the information had been noted, each one would be destroyed.

In the next few days, 40 Chinese in Tanjong Malim were arrested; and soon the restrictions were lifted. Before long 3,500 of the people in the district joined the Home Guard. The guerrilla platoon that had conducted the ambush split up and left the area, and for the remaining eight years of the war Tanjong Malim had one of the most peaceful records in the country.

---

[2] Miller, *op. cit.*, p. 209.

The extent to which these developments were brought about by the collective punishment and the sealed-box information, on the one hand, and the intensified army and police effort, on the other, can never be assessed. Far more important, however, was the effect in other towns and villages throughout the federation. Templer was firmly in the saddle, and everyone knew it.

Though he was personally responsible for every aspect of government, Templer spent little time in Kuala Lumpur, preferring to keep his judgment sharp and realistic by visiting the villages, the police posts, the infantry battalions, and the DWEC's. To do this, he left much of the day-to-day administration to his two deputies, Sir Donald MacGillivray on the government side and General Sir Rob Lockhart as Deputy Director of Operations. Under them were the Executive Council and the Director of Operations' Committee, respectively. Though these two groups gradually changed their composition and their titles as the country advanced through self-government to independence, they continued to exist with essentially the same functions until the war was over. The Executive Council, a civil body, included the responsible ministers and the Security Force commanders as members. The other was an operational executive body, in which the Security Force commanders directed the war, with senior civil servants from the Defense and Information departments taking part.

For his function as Director of Operations, Templer had an astonishingly small staff. Started by Briggs, it was retained by Templer and his successors. Excluding his aides, it never exceeded nine officers. Headed by his deputy (later renamed the principal staff officer), its main element was a team of four officers of lieutenant colonel level—a soldier, an airman, a policeman, and a civil servant. These four, like the General himself, traveled frequently, leaving the principal staff officer and three junior staff officers in Kuala Lumpur. When they visited SWEC's and DWEC's, they attended as a team that mirrored the composition of the committees themselves; they were able to make decisions or accept action on the Director of Operations' behalf on any problem that might arise, from troop reinforcements and air support to rice rationing and road development.

They also spent much of their time visiting units on the ground; in particular, they visited those who were killing a large number of guerrillas, to find out how they did it. The explanation for a high kill-rate usually was good intelligence information, which in turn depended on confidence and cooperation between the soldiers and the Special Branch. The staff officers' task was to see what techniques were working out well on the ground, so that they could be applied elsewhere. Because there were no intervening staff levels, there were very few briefings, papers, or written reports; the officers would go from the DWEC or the jungle directly to the general, tell him what they had seen, and the general would reply with his decisions, on the spot. Since the staff was joint, this was all that was needed. The four members could get his decisions put into effect without delay through police, air, or army headquarters, or the appropriate ministry. It was simple and quick, leaving the officers free to set out the next day for another area.

Thus the job of the staff members was not to develop bright ideas of their own. The ideas were there in plenty among the people actually fighting the guerrillas. The staff's function was to find out about these ideas and choose which ones to develop.

Templer set the example. He was a great listener, particularly to the people with ideas, the policemen, platoon commanders, district officers, and rubber planters. He had a direct manner and an inquiring mind that appealed to them. He found out what they wanted, promised to get it for them, and did. He was also quick to spot faults. Weak commanders or officials who could not work together found themselves packing their bags.

He also had a long memory, and an efficient means of prompting it. He was always accompanied by his military assistant, David Lloyd Owen, a young infantry officer with a fine combat record and a brain as sharp as Templer's. In the course of a half-hour visit, personalities, problems, and faults would be noted, and the general was reminded of them as he approached the place on his next visit, usually about three months later. The people would first be surprised to be recognized, astounded by his memory of the details of their problems—and in real trouble if any fault which had been noted last time had not been put right.

Although Templer is remembered first as a man of action, perhaps his greatest strength was his readiness to take risks with the Chinese. His trust was strictly pragmatic; he knew that most of the Chinese, despite their racial ties with the guerrillas, would be glad to see the war over. He particularly trusted the Home Guard, which was formed under the Briggs Plan in every village and kampong. The Malay kampongs by this time could look after their own defense, releasing all their police for duty elsewhere. This was no great risk, since the guerrillas, having learned to expect no help from the Malays, generally left them alone. Templer, however, placed increasing trust in the Home Guard in the Chinese New Villages. As guardsmen, they would have access to weapons, learn how to use them, and receive training in the technique of commanding fighting soldiers. When a Communist was unmasked in the Home Guard, he was usually one of the best men, sometimes the platoon commander. Templer knew the risk. The price had to be paid, but it proved to be a small one. The dividends were far, far greater.

He tried to create the same attitude of trust between the Malay police and the Chinese villagers. This was not easy; hostility between them dated from the Japanese occupation. The Malay constables were referred to by the Chinese as *"mata-mata,"* which means "eyes"—twelve pairs of government eyes spying on them in their village. To help him improve this image, Templer borrowed the City of London Police Comissioner, Colonel A. E. Young, who launched an "Operation Service" campaign. Outside every police post, he put a sign showing a pair of clasped hands and the word "service" in the appropriate languages. The campaign's effect was less on the Chinese villagers than on the constables, whose morale improved when they saw themselves as friends, not enemies, of the villagers.

Templer knew that no victory would be permanent unless the government won over many of the Chinese. He knew that to gain their confidence, the government had to free them from the fear of Communist violence, as the penalty for cooperating with authority. To end this threat, the village police had to stop the terrorist murders and the soldiers had to kill more guerrillas and to let the people see that these things were being done.

Killing guerrillas meant finding them, and the focus of the war shifted from security to police intelligence.

# 10

## ACROSS THE JUNGLE FRINGE

By the spring of 1952, the government campaign had swung over to the offensive, and the whole character of the war had changed. Until the end of 1951, the strategy had inevitably been defensive, first to prevent a *coup d'état,* and then to prevent an erosion of government control in the villages that would spread to districts and regions. Thanks to the Briggs Plan, the rural Chinese were now relatively secure at night in their New Villages and the village police posts could confidently resist the raids of the guerrilla platoons.

These platoons, however, were far more difficult to find than the old company and regimental groups; indeed, that is why they had split up. As Chin Peng's directive of October, 1951, was put into effect by his units, it became almost impossible to find them except by means of information from the people in the New Villages.

The people, however, had little direct contact with the fighting platoons, except as victims of raids of which they had no prior knowledge. Their contacts were with the Communists' parallel hierarchy—the political and supply organization—and it was against this that the government's main offensive effort was directed from the spring of 1952 onward.

The political and supply organization of the Malayan Communist Party (MCP) is shown in Figure 3. It consisted of the Central Committee (or Politburo) with its family tree of state or regional committees, district committees, and branch committees. Each of the branch committees was supported by guerrilla working parties (known as armed work forces). The branch committees and the armed work forces gradually merged, and the two will hereafter be referred to as the MCP branches. Their duty was to control and keep contact with the People's Organization, the Minh Yuen, in their villages. Before the Briggs Plan took effect, many of the MCP branches lived fairly freely among the squatters on the jungle fringe; but due to resettlement and the Emergency Regulations, they were by 1951 all living beyond the jungle fringe, maintaining their clandestine government of the villages through contacts with their Minh Yuen representatives either at work in the fields or in the villages at night.

The parallel hierarchy not only "governed" the villages but also obtained supplies for the Malayan Races' Liberation Army (MRLA) platoons, whose operations (under the October, 1951, directive) were geared specifically to enforcing obedience to its rule.

In 1951, 8,000 armed guerrillas were in the jungle. During the subsequent six years, their casualties (9,000) greatly exceeded their recruits (3,000); and their strength fell to 2,000 in 1957.

It is, however, the breakdown of these figures between the fighting units and the political and supply organization that is significant:

|  | Numbers | | Percentages | |
|---|---|---|---|---|
|  | *1951* | *1957* | *1951* | *1957* |
| MRLA fighting units | 5,500 | 200 | 70 | 10 |
| MCP political and supply organization | 2,500 | 1,800 | 30 | 90 |
| TOTAL GUERRILLA STRENGTH | 8,000 | 2,000 | 100 | 100 |

FIGURE 3
THE PARALLEL HIERARCHY

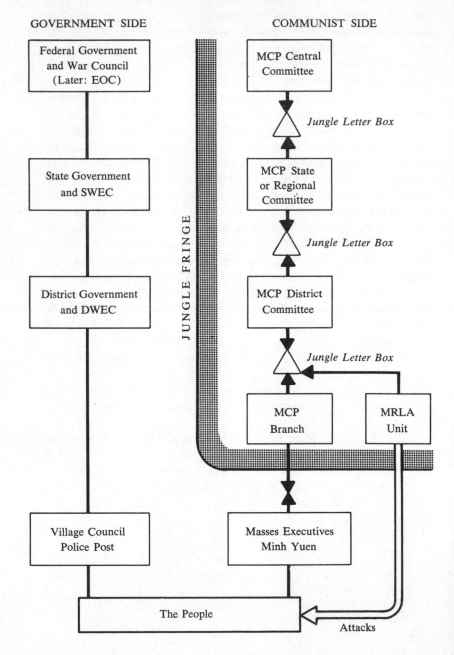

The MRLA fighting strength fell during these years because Templer and his successors so decimated the political and supply organization, particularly the MCP branches, that the fighting units had to be milked to keep the branches going. Thus, by 1957, the MCP was forced to employ 90 per cent of its men in branch duties; for if any MCP branch ceased to be viable, the village for which it was responsible would be without a Communist parallel government—and in that village the cause would be lost.

Communication between the MCP Central Committee and state or regional, district, and branch committees was by courier.[1]

In the early months of the insurgency, the courier system had been reasonably quick and efficient because, as in Vietnam, the couriers had lived outside the jungle and carried the messages by road or sent them through the post. Even the higher committees had lived close enough to the jungle fringe to be accessible to couriers in the squatters' areas. By 1952, however, resettlement, registration, and police checks made it too difficult for these couriers to move by road; and army patrols had driven the higher committees deeper into the jungle. Improved police intelligence had made the committees so fearful of betrayal that they kept their camp locations secret, both from the supporters outside and from each other. They kept touch only through a tenuous system of jungle couriers and letter boxes.

Each MCP branch had a courier, who knew the location of the district letter box but not of the district camp. The branch courier called at the letter box every two weeks to leave and collect messages. The district courier also called, but on different days; so the two couriers never met. The camps, harassed by patrols, moved often; but the letter box remained fixed. Only the couriers and a few high-ranking Communists knew where these letter boxes were, but even these officials did not know the day-to-day locations of the camps; if they wanted to visit a branch committee they could do so only by going to the letter box on the appropriate day and getting the branch courier to guide them back to his camp. If it was

---

[1] The guerrillas made occasional attempts to use radio, but the humid conditions, mountainous terrain, and difficulty in getting spare parts made radio an unreliable means of communication for them.

suspected that the letter box itself was compromised, intense precautions were taken in switching the couriers to a new one.

This system of communications was so slow that directives from the MCP Central Committee often took six months to filter down through state and district committees to branch committees and MRLA platoons. For example, Chin Peng's October, 1951, directive clearly had not reached the platoon that destroyed the Tanjong Malim water supply in March, 1952.

Later in the war, we occasionally located these jungle letter boxes, through information supplied by surrendered guerrillas; when we did, the very secrecy of the system enabled us to reap spectacular dividends. Our primary intelligence, however, came from the MCP branch committees' regular contacts with their supporters from the villages.

The clandestine organization in the Chinese villages was run on the Communist cell system. It was led by masses executives, the senior Communists living in the village. In a village of about 1,000, there usually would be a half-dozen executives—one each responsible for supplies, finance, propaganda, intelligence, security, and traitor elimination. They would live normal lives as rubber tappers, coffee-shop proprietors, barbers, or taxi drivers. Through contact men in cells throughout the village, they would control the activity of 100 or more villagers willing (or compelled) to perform such chores as collecting money, making guerrilla uniforms, and smuggling food. In some areas, almost everyone in the village was blackmailed into contributing money to the Communists as the price of being allowed to work unmolested. Those who did not pay might find themselves without work because the rubber trees had been slashed; some who did not pay were slashed to death themselves. The more prosperous villagers—shopkeepers and bus or truck owners—might have to contribute hundreds of dollars a month to keep their property intact.

The masses executives usually were Party members, and so were a few of their active supporters. Whether such members worked in the jungle or in the villages depended on whether they were (or thought they were) suspected by the police. If a good Communist was likely to be free from arrest, he could do far more for the movement inside the village than outside. At the first whiff of suspicion, however, he would be off to the jungle. The branch would have a new member, and the remaining executives would promote another trusted villager to handle his department.

Figure 4 shows a typical rubber plantation, supporting a population of 5,000 resettled into 5 Chinese villages, each containing its Malay police post. In the area lived a company of infantry soldiers, of whom at any given time a few would be resting in camp, ready to support the police if they were raided. The others were out on patrol, checking passes in the rubber; watching for suspicious movements; living for days or weeks in the jungle, hoping to spot contacts between the guerrillas and the rubber tappers or at least to gather shreds of evidence from which the police Special Branch could build up an intelligence picture that might lead to the recruiting of an agent. Sometimes, by spotting tracks, hearing movement, or getting a tip-off, the soldiers sprang a successful ambush and killed a few guerrillas.

Operating in competition with the soldiers, as shown in Figure 4, were two guerrilla units, an independent MRLA platoon (thirty strong) and the MCP branch (fifteen). The platoon in fact was a district unit, operating in four or five branch areas. When it was to make a raid, it contacted the local branch through the district courier system and was guided to a suitable camp site near the jungle fringe. The branch then provided it with supplies and an intelligence briefing. The platoon and section commanders were given a rendezvous to meet guides to take them on reconnaissance, possibly also to meet a masses executive from the target village if the raid was to be coordinated with action in the village (for instance, to cut telephone wires, divert the police, or give light signals). The desired dividends of the raid were a haul of weapons and ammunition, a live-and-let-live police post, and a better-disciplined population.

The platoon could do nothing without the branch. It could get no food, information, or guides. And the branch could get these only from its five Chinese villages. If any Malay kampongs were in the area, the branch ignored them because it would get no help from them, and any visit would certainly be reported to the police.

The branch contacted its supporters at work in the rubber or, as on the right of Figure 4, in logging areas of the jungle. Sometimes these contacts were by prior arrangement, but usually they were not. Sometimes the branch simply had the masses executives

FIGURE 4

AN MCP BRANCH AND ITS SUPPORTERS

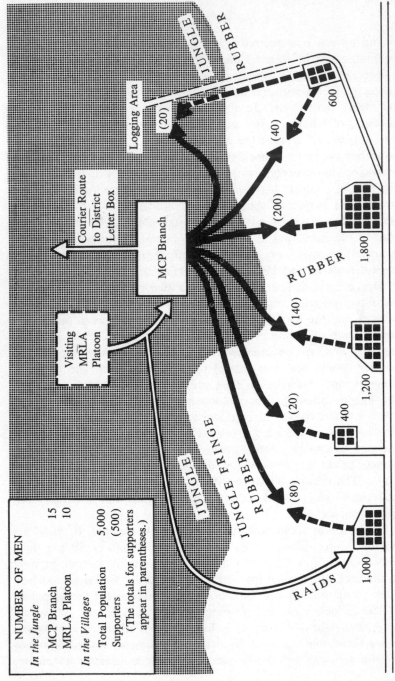

NUMBER OF MEN

*In the Jungle*

MCP Branch        15
MRLA Platoon      10

*In the Villages*

Total Population   5,000
Supporters          (500)
(The totals for supporters appear in parentheses.)

Courier Route to District Letter Box

Logging Area

Visiting MRLA Platoon

MCP Branch

JUNGLE

RUBBER

JUNGLE

JUNGLE FRINGE

RUBBER

RUBBER

RAIDS

(20)

(40)

(200)

(140)

(20)

(80)

600

1,800

1,200

400

1,000

Infantry Company Camp

organize the dumping of food in prearranged hiding places, and the branch collected it when convenient. This method was the safest against ambush. The methods varied, depending on the activity of the police and army patrols, the audacity of the branch committee secretary, and the degree to which he knew and trusted his supporters.

It was from among these supporters that the police Special Branch recruited its village agents. In the defended Chinese villages, about 10 per cent of the population was actively and willingly supporting the guerrillas. A few of these supporters were dedicated Communists. Others were being loyal to the guerrilla army that had opposed the Japanese and was still fighting foreign soldiers and Malays. Others had friends or relatives in the jungle. (Whatever her politics, it was no surprise if a mother smuggled food to her son, even though she faced years in jail if caught.) No matter what the reason, however, these supporters could not be turned into agents.

Another part of the population, also about 10 per cent, was definitely anti-Communist. These persons, as a rule, were the successful ones, who had good prospects of making money—shopkeepers, garage mechanics, taxi drivers, or rubber tappers looking forward to saving enough money to start a business of their own. These people are the lifeblood of a free economy, and the Chinese are better than most races at breeding them. This type certainly had no desire to see their economic ambitions thwarted by the Communists, and they were prepared to help prevent this. They were not, however, suitable as police agents, since they seldom would be accepted into the ranks of the Communist supporters and would not therefore have access to their secrets.

The villagers with no strong feelings either way, the other 80 per cent, wished only to see the war over and until then to keep out of trouble with either side. Faced with police checks, curfews, and the threat of fines and imprisonment, they did their best to comply with government regulations, though they dared not admit to having seen any guerrillas. On the other hand, faced by a guerrilla with a gun, they did what he told them to, if they thought the police were lax enough for them to get away with it.

Rubber tapping was a lonely job. A good tapper could deal with 300 or even 500 trees in a day. He (or she) visited each tree twice —once to cut the bark and fix the latex cup to catch the drips, and then again three or four hours later to empty the cup into a tin. Each operation took about five seconds—three or four hours to cut the bark of all the trees, another three or four hours to empty the cups, with periodic visits to the weighing shed to hand in the latex and be credited with his pay, so many cents to the pound. In the area of the trees tapped by one worker, covering perhaps five acres, not another person was to be seen—unless an army patrol came by and asked to see his pass or half-a-dozen armed guerrillas with red stars on their caps and guns in their hands emerged from the jungle fringe and asked him if he were "a friend of the people." At their first visit, the guerrillas from the branch (or maybe a per-suasive masses executive who had walked over from the neighboring rubber lot) might be quite gentle and friendly, saying that the boys in the jungle were hungry and needed cigarettes, and asking if he could help. When he did, they would be duly grateful, while urging him to bring a bit more the next time, and maybe some medical supplies or a shirt that the tailor on the corner would give him. He would soon be "committed." If he ever tried to back off, there would be threats of violence or hints that evidence of his "crimes" might be leaked to the police—or maybe a threat of some more direct and violent punishment.

These persons did not help the Communists because they wanted to, and they were only too ready to get out of it if they could be offered a safe means of doing so. Therein lay our chance, and we took it. We aimed first to identify the willing supporters (the 10 per cent) and arrest them, forcing the guerrillas to rely more and more on the coerced ones. Then we aimed to identify these to find likely men (or girls) to turn into agents.

# 11

# INTELLIGENCE AGENTS—
# FACT AND FANTASY

Hㅤow does an intelligence service recruit its agents? And how does it guard against betrayal by double agents?

By "agents," I do not mean the ordinary paid informers who contribute the mass of minor details that build up the general picture of the enemy and his movements. These informers can give information only about what they see and hear. An agent is a trusted member of the enemy organization who is willing to betray its secrets to us; he can give the specific information that wins the battles in this kind of war.

Many people think that the majority of such agents are "inserted" by training a man who speaks the language and sending him to join the Communists in Southeast Asia. There is normally only one credible cover plan for this kind of agent: to represent himself as a defector from our side who is willing to work as an agent for the Communists. We feed him enough information to keep their trust while he finds out their secrets and tells them to us. This is the storybook agent. In practice, he is potentially—if not actually —a double agent. Experience with double agents suggests that, when under pressure, they will jump to whichever side will save their neck or pay them most. The Communists have been plagued with them from the earliest days of their movement, and their "bibles" are full of warnings about them. Anyone we try to insert in this way will be kept under particular scrutiny, however appetizing his initial contributions may seem to be. Though some such insertions from outside the country have been achieved (Lai Tek may have been inserted, as described in Chapter 1), these agents are very risky, and their number represents such a minute proportion of the total number of intelligence agents that we need not consider them further.

Inserting a local man, born and raised in the area, is much easier. But the Communists are intensely alive to this possibility; if there is the slightest question about his motives in joining them, or about his past, they treat him with great reserve.

Many local men were recruited as informers in Malaya, of course. They could tell the police whom they saw in their areas of work, watch a particular house, or notice who talked to whom in the coffee shop. That was valuable intelligence, but it was the knowledge of what was going to happen *in the future* that put the guerrillas into the sights of the soldiers' rifles. We called this "contact information," and usually it came only from a delicately handled agent who was privy to the Communists' plans.

We recruited almost all our agents from among people who had begun to work for the Communists from genuine motives, with no intention of becoming police agents. Many of them had been coerced by the Communists; and indeed, some measure of coercion was also necessary on our side before many of them would accept the risk of becoming our agents.

The first step in spotting prospects was to separate the Communists' political and supply organization from the people by forcing the guerrillas into the jungle; we did this through the Emergency Regulations described in Chapter 5. The second step was to make it dangerous for the villagers to contact the guerrillas, so that only the dedicated or heavily blackmailed suppliers would take the risk. We then identified as many of these contacts as possible and arrested those who we believed were doing it willingly. The fourth step was to pinpoint one or two of the coerced contacts whose allegiance might be shifted to our side without exciting Communist suspicion.

We found that the contacts easiest to spot were those supplying food. This also applies in certain areas of South Vietnam, mainly north of Saigon, where food is short, and where the local administration and police work are efficient enough to make it reasonably difficult for the Viet Cong to smuggle food out of the villages. There are other areas where food control is impracticable: the Mekong and Red River deltas in Vietnam and the paddy-growing areas of northern Malaya. In those areas of Malaya, we concentrated instead on other points of contact between the guerrillas and the village population, for political indoctrination, propaganda, intelligence, or the supply of necessities other than food (weapons, ammunition, explosives, medical supplies, and clothing).

Once identified, the man who had been coerced into keeping in regular touch with the Communists was given plenty of rope; evidence was built up against him without letting him realize he was being watched. When the police had enough evidence, a Chinese plain-clothes officer or detective of the Special Branch made secret contact with the man, waylaying him some dark night in his village and driving him out to some remote spot in the woods for interrogation.

To some people, the word "interrogation" conjures up visions of red-hot pokers. Torture is, in fact, the most shortsighted method of trying to get information; however great the immediate dividends may seem to be, they are always more than paid for by the losses in the long run—as the Germans, Russians, and French have found in their own attempts to defeat guerrillas. This is not only because torture is immoral, and must eventually turn the people against us, but also because, although torture may induce the victim to tell us what happened yesterday or even what is going to happen tonight, it will not make him into an agent who will keep up his contacts with the Communists and betray them to us.

The Special Branch interrogation technique was much more subtle than a red-hot poker. The victim sat in the dark in the passenger seat of a parked car, too far from help to call out, as the Special Branch man spelled out the damning evidence against him.

"On June 10, Ah Yau, you had a pound of rice concealed in a false bottom in your latex tin. We saw it. On June 20, you went out to work with a pair of khaki trousers wrapped around your stomach under your shirt. On June 30, you went out wearing a new pair of shoes, with an old pair stuffed in your pocket. We saw them, and we also saw you coming back that same evening wearing the old ones. What did you do with those new shoes? And last week, Ah Yau, you bought seven rounds of rifle ammunition from Constable Abdul Hamid. There's not much need to deny it, because we have a tape recording of your conversation in the coffee shop with Abdul Hamid. And two other constables will testify that they removed those cartridges from the hole you dug in your tapioca patch. We have a photograph of them doing it, and your fingerprints are on the cartridges."

Ah Yau would deny the charges, of course: "It must be someone else. I would never supply the Communists. I hate the Communists. They murdered my best friend." But he knew it was all true, just as the Special Branch officer was saying; and even if he talked his way out of this charge, he could not hope to go on supplying the guerrillas. The next time he would be arrested red-handed.

He could not go on, but neither could he stop. If he did, the Communists would guess that it was because he was under suspicion; they would kill him before he could talk. He would be found tied to a rubber tree, his neck torn apart with a shovel, covered with blood and with a notice warning others of the fate of a "Traitor to the People." He had seen too many bodies like that to have any illusions about it.

But there was, of course, a way out. He could admit the charges, claiming that he had acted under coercion, and promise to help the police. Then, at the first opportunity, he could escape through the jungle fringe and become a guerrilla. Indeed, once the war was in its stride, the main source of recruits for the guerrillas were supporters who found themselves in fear of arrest.

If the Special Branch had chosen its victim well, however, he would have good reasons not to go into the jungle—a family, a small business, old age, or poor health. And so, Ah Yau would plead for a fourth alternative: protective arrest. But this request would be refused.

By insinuation, the Special Branch man would sow in Ah Yau's mind the only sensible course open to him: to go on working for the Communists but to tell the police when he next arranged to meet them so that they could be ambushed and killed. The interrogator would remind him of the rewards for information leading to the capture and death of a guerrilla—12,000 Malayan dollars (U.S. $4,000) for a district committee member. Ah Yau knew it would take him ten years to earn that much as a rubber tapper.

Thus, Ah Yau would become a police agent. Having once taken this decision, he would work with increasing cunning and determination, with one object: to help wipe out the guerrilla branch members, who were now, so long as they remained at large, a terrible threat to his life. Then he could collect his reward and be on his way, with his family and his money, leaving all this terror behind him, to start a new life under a new name, in Hong Kong or Thailand or Sarawak.

The Special Branch played a delicate role. One agent could cause a successful ambush that would boost local confidence. This would lead to more information, more ambushes, and then to a trickle of surrenders. Surrendered guerrillas were widely used by the police in the interrogation of others, and also in persuading suppliers to become agents.

But first find your agent.

In every Chinese village of any size, there was a plain-clothes Special Branch detective, usually a corporal or sergeant. Supervising each group of three or four villages was a police inspector. In charge of the district was an assistant superintendent; and at the top was the Director of Special Branch, at Federal Police Headquarters. Many of the higher Special Branch officers were British; but at the bottom level, where the battle for the mind of each potential agent was fought, the officers were almost invariably Malayan Chinese.

These plain-clothes detectives lived in the local police post. Their identity was well known to the Communists, so they were particular targets for assassination. Their ranks were also an attractive target for Communist penetration. They had to be trustworthy, able to keep the identity of their particular agents to themselves, and, in these conditions of great secrecy, to negotiate rewards that made their own salaries look small. The opportunities for corruption were tremendous, so these men were handpicked. The inspectors, who did most of the interrogation of prospective agents, were often young Chinese college graduates.

The lack of a singleminded and reliable intelligence organization at village level has been one of the most serious defects in the war in South Vietnam. The root of the problem has been the lack of a secure police and local government organization within which a police intelligence officer could operate. A single "secret police-man" for intelligence work is most unlikely ever to get his hands on a potential agent who is trusted by the Communists, or to per-suade him to betray them; to do this, he needs to be in possession of the mass of low-grade information that comes from a large number of casual informers. This means that a lot of people in the village must know him for what he is; and under present con-ditions in South Vietnam, he would probably not stay alive very long. Special Branch did not begin to operate effectively in the Malayan Chinese villages until the police posts had been made secure in 1951, and this must be the first step to any real progress in counterinsurgency.

Another problem in South Vietnam has been that the repeated political and military coups have caused the intelligence organiza-tions to devote more effort to watching each other than to watching the Viet Cong.

Though we never had to face this kind of instability in Malaya, we did suffer in the early days from mistrust and lack of coordina-tion between the army and police intelligence services. We solved this by our system of SWEC's and DWEC's (see Chapter 7). After 1951, all Communist intelligence was handled and controlled by the police Special Branch, with the other agencies working to support it.

There is no doubt that the soundest (and, in the end, the cheapest) investment against Communist insurgency in any coun-try is in a strong, handpicked, and well-paid police intelligence organization, backed by the funds to offer good rewards.

# 12

## SURRENDERED ENEMY PERSONNEL
## (SEP's)

THE two young Malayan Chinese made a striking contrast as they faced each other across the table: a Special Branch officer, clean and alert, and a surrendered guerrilla in tattered uniform, dirty and hungry, but at the same time strangely elated.

"Your name?"

"Kum Sun."

"Where is your camp?"

"About two hours' march into the jungle, by a stream. It's hard to describe."

"Can you lead us to it?"

"Yes."

"Now?"

"Yes."

The Special Branch officer nodded to his detective sergeant, who went off to telephone the army patrol that was already standing by.

"How long ago did you leave the camp?"

"About four hours."

"Do they know you have surrendered?"

"No. We were on a food-collecting job. We thought we heard a patrol and left the track. We got separated. They'll just think I'm lost."

"When will they suspect?"

"Maybe if I'm not back by morning."

"And then they will move?"

"Yes."

"But you can take us there in the dark? Now?"

"Yes."

Kum Sun led the patrol to the camp, gave the password to the sentry, and silently strangled him. The patrol surrounded the sleeping camp. Kum Sun walked in, put a pistol to the head of his leader, and fired. This was the signal for the patrol to charge and seize the rest of the guerrillas.

There were many stories like this one in Malaya. It amazed the British soldiers that the Chinese guerrillas could creep up on sleeping former comrades, with whom they had lived through years of hardship in the jungle, and kill them. But they needed little encouragement and certainly none of the "torture" by which Communist propaganda tried to account for their treachery. After about five years, we began to understand these surrendered enemy personnel (SEP's, as we called them); but perhaps our very understanding was a reminder of the gulf that divides the Western and the Chinese minds.[1]

The newly surrendered (or captured) guerrillas were dirty, unkempt, and exhausted; they were undernourished, pale from lack of sunshine under the jungle canopy, and weakened by festering sores from the bites of insects and leeches. After a few weeks of good food and clean living conditions, however, they looked very different. Most were intelligent and alert. The overriding impres-

---

[1] A major contribution was made in this field by Dr. Lucian Pye, who in 1952–53 conducted exhaustive interviews with sixty surrendered guerrillas in Malaya, to find out why they had joined and why they had surrendered. His findings are published in his *Guerrilla Communism in Malaya*, which I found invaluable while I was in Malaya.

sion was that, disconcerted with what life had to offer them, they had joined the guerrillas to try to do something positive about it.

There were exceptions. Some were fugitives from justice; others had been blackmailed into joining by the Communists, who got them involved in smuggling supplies and then threatened to betray them to the police. Most guerrillas of this type were employed only as carriers, cooks, and cannon fodder; and even in those humble roles, they were a dubious asset, often merely adding to the number of surrenders and thereby to the flow of intelligence. Such men were, however, a minority.

It is a common and dangerous error to underestimate the quality of Communist guerrillas. In Malaya, the education of the Communist guerrillas was generally above the average. Although they grew up amid the administrative chaos of the Japanese occupation, many of them had spent six years in school. This was often one of the causes of the frustration that had driven them into becoming Communists. Most of them had lived in villages where the only work was tapping rubber. They wanted something better. Many of the younger generation in the towns were no less frustrated. Some had left their villages in the hope of a better life, but they could get only menial jobs. The Communists seemed to offer them the opportunity to get somewhere, to be someone.

They took to the jungle with high hopes, which often remained high for two or three years. Lack of promotion usually set off the process of disillusion. Some began to sense defeat. They had joined the party because they thought they would ride with it to victory and power; but after a couple of years in the jungle, they realized they were being hunted and harried by better soldiers who beat them every time they met. They did not like losing six men for every soldier and policeman they killed.

They received little encouragement from the villagers, who greeted them not as liberators but as burdens on the backs of the people. Weary of being the raw material of a war, first between guerrillas and Japanese, and now between guerrillas and British and Malays, the people contributed to the Party funds, but there was no joy in the response and no emotional reward for the young men who longed to lead.

Even the guerrillas' personal friendships with other guerrillas soon became stultified; the strict and dreary procedures of Communism killed their feelings of comradeship. The weekly mutual criticism meetings were fine at first, but bit by bit, they bred distrust and suspicion. If a man were the subject of official censure, his closest friends dared not be seen chatting with him, and he was intensely lonely even in the confines of a tiny camp. The young recruits learned that no true friendship could survive in the atmosphere of a secret revolutionary movement. They were spending the best years of their lives in a miserable existence to aid a cause that was doomed to failure.

Once the guerrilla began to lose heart, his hatred for Communism would grow. The Party had misled him and brought him hardship and danger to no purpose. It was wasting his life; worse, it had made a fool of him. If he went back to his family, he would have to admit he had been wrong. Many Chinese would rather die than lose face—and many did. While the disillusioned guerrilla awaited his opportunity to surrender, his hatred centered on the Party's representatives, particularly his own MCP branch leader and the men who supported him. He knew that if these men suspected his true thoughts for a moment, they would kill him. It seemed quite logical to him to kill them instead.

The government offered generous surrender terms. Besides the large rewards for helping to kill or capture other guerrillas, there were various amnesty terms at different times in the emergency. The most effective were those in the Merdeka (Freedom) Offer leaflets showered into the jungle after the independence celebrations in August, 1957, on the reverse side of leaflets bearing a safe-conduct pass in English, Malay, Tamil, and Chinese. The terms read:

1. Those of you who genuinely desire to give up the armed struggle may come out of the jungle and may ask any individual to help you to do this.
2. You must bring your arms with you or be prepared to state where they are so that they can be recovered by the Government.
3. You will NOT be prosecuted for any offense connected with the emergency which you have committed under Communist direction before this date.
4. Those who show that they genuinely intend to be loyal to the elected Government of Malaya and to give up their Communist

activities will be helped to regain their normal life and to be reunited with their families, if they so wish.

5. As regards the remainder, they will be repatriated to China (with their families if they so wish) and will not be made the subject of any investigation but will be given fair treatment while awaiting repatriation.[2]

The practice of amnesty had, however, gone further even than the printed word on these leaflets. By 1957, the guerrillas, were generally aware that no one who surrendered on his own initiative had been prosecuted. Moreover, even guerrillas captured in battle were never prosecuted if they cooperated with the government against their ex-comrades.[3] If caught in possession of a weapon, however, a guerrilla faced a death sentence; for under the Emergency Regulations, he was legally regarded not as a soldier but as a criminal. But only in extreme cases was the death sentence carried out. If there was any spark of cooperation, the captured guerrilla was reclassified as an SEP. This certainly paid off, encouraging guerrillas both to surrender and to cooperate.

The psychological-warfare campaign expanded as the war progressed. "Voice aircraft" flying over the jungle often broadcast taped messages from members of local units who had surrendered, telling the guerrillas that they were wasting their lives, that they would be well treated if they surrendered, and that life out of the jungle was good. Leaflets were dropped carrying two photographs of a guerrilla—one taken at the time of his surrender, scrawny and exhausted; another taken a few weeks later, plump and smiling, with his mother and his girl friend, standing in front of the family

---

[2] Significantly, very few of the surrendered enemy personnel elected to be repatriated to China. One wonders how those who did were treated when they got there!

[3] The Communists did not offer even this alternative to captured British or Gurkha soldiers, whom they killed on the spot. However, they sometimes released Malays, especially policemen. Lenient treatment of prisoners, a sound investment in guerrilla warfare, is specifically recommended by Mao Tse-tung. Castro followed the same precept. He used to invite any captured Batista troops to join his side; if they declined, he would usually let them go free with a contemptuous warning: "Fight us again if you like. Next time you may be killed in the battle, but if not we will capture you again—and then will let you go again. You don't frighten us at all." On an army whose morale was already low, this contempt had a considerable psychological effect.

table stacked high with food. Apart from the suggestion that the Communists had misled them into wasting their lives, politics was not even mentioned.

Government psychological-warfare material was written by Chinese, including a number of ex-Communists. The team was led by a forceful and imaginative Malayan Chinese, C. C. Too, who spent much time talking to surrendered guerrillas and studying captured documents. He was adept at forecasting their policies and reactions, and his psychological-warfare approach was based on the understanding gained from this constant contact with current Communist thinking. It took us some time to learn the obvious lesson that psychological warfare *must* be directed by a local man. It is amazing how many Europeans think they understand the Asian mind. The really able Europeans, however, realized that their function was to provide good organization and enough supervision to insure against corruption and treachery, and to leave the intellectual contacts with Chinese guerrillas and villagers—both in the police Special Branch and psychological warfare—to other Chinese.

Psychological warfare alone, however, could not produce surrendered guerrillas. A few surrenders were "negotiated" by agents or by near relatives among the suppliers (with the usual rewards), but the great majority came from areas under intense military pressure. This was partly because of the danger and hardship of the life of a hunted man—narrow escapes, hunger, and the disruption of the rather pathetic little comforts that soldiers create for themselves when campaigning in the jungle. If the guerrilla was already beset by doubts about the future, and about whether the people wanted him to liberate them anyway, these dangers and heartbreaks were harder to bear.

The Communist leaders were well aware that surrender was the most devastating disease that could strike their army. The MCP therefore made it a capital offense even to pick up a government surrender leaflet. Still more compelling was the control that the Communists established over their men's minds by their self-criticism technique. It was very hard for a guerrilla even to contemplate surrender without an uneasy feeling that "they" would find out; he flinched from the idea of thinking out a definite plan for escape. It was far easier to sit, wet, miserable, and hungry, and do nothing. Many unhappy guerrillas did just that, for years, in the later stages of the war, until forceful pestering by soldiers with guns became even more unbearable.

Without military pressure, then, there were no surrenders. But once the first few SEP's came in, their information and cooperation led to more pressure by the army, which led to more narrow escapes, more kills, and more surrenders—a kind of galloping consumption that was fatal.

After his months of agony and indecision, culminating in the tension of taking the plunge, the surrendered guerrilla's relief at being safely in the police station exploded into a wave of intensely high spirits. With hundreds of friendly soldiers all around, amid unanswerable proofs of affluence and power, he felt for the moment a sense of invincibility. He took little persuading to stride back into the jungle, wielding the overwhelming military force now at his disposal, to obliterate forever the gang that had held him for so long in its clutches. The technique therefore was to take him out with a patrol immediately, before this enthusiasm had waned and before his unit had moved—as they certainly would as soon as they suspected that he had surrendered. It was also very desirable to compromise him at once (i.e., to make him do some unforgivable damage to the MCP), particularly if there were any risk that he might be a plant, or if he were a captured guerrilla "agreeing" to cooperate.

In the early days after his surrender, an SEP would often react strongly to the feeling that he was trusted. One of our most brilliant guerrilla fighters, Major F. E. Kitson, gave a convincing demonstration of this. Having captured two guerrillas in the afternoon, he persuaded them to help him to find the rest of their gang. He took them out just before dark, and they camped in the jungle for the night. The two SEP's were astounded when they were given rifles and placed on sentry duty while Kitson and his patrol slept at their mercy.

Kitson had a particular flair for handling SEP's.[4] Indeed, his

---

[4] Kitson came to Malaya having been a highly successful and unconventional intelligence officer in Kenya, where he formed surrendered Mau-Mau into "pseudogangs" whom he accompanied (with a blackened face) into the villages to terrify them into telling all they knew of other Mau-Mau gangs, with whom the pseudogangs would then make a rendezvous for the kill. He has described this technique in *Gangs and Counter-gangs* (London: Barrie and Rockliff, 1960).

clearing of one district into which he moved as a company commander was outstanding. The previous company had reduced the guerrillas to considerable misery but had few agents and no surrenders. Kitson at once turned his whole company to intelligence work. He distributed them in twos and threes around the rubber and logging tracks to watch the faces of the people going to work until they could recognize any strangers among them. After a few weeks, they had provided enough clues for the Special Branch to start interrogating. They got no agents, but they did get one interesting bit of information—that the MCP branch, which they knew lived on the opposite side of a road through the jungle, was so short of supplies that it had begun to cross over the road from time to time to pick up more; it was expected to come again very soon. Kitson, knowing this road and jungle well by then, deduced that the guerrillas would cross at night using one of six trails. He ambushed all the trails every night until he killed one guerrilla and captured another. This man led them back, and they killed another. The gang, scared of further betrayal, began to break up. Other surrenders led to mounting pressure; eventually, after six months, every MCP branch, district, and platoon in the area had been eliminated. Finally, with neither troops nor a hierarchy left to direct, the MCP state committee secretary came in to surrender with his personal staff of seven. That was the end of the war for another forty villages.

In this case, the Communist leader was tough and held out until all his men had surrendered. It was more profitable if a leader (MCP branch or district committee member and higher) could be captured alive or induced to surrender early; this almost invariably resulted in a rapid collapse of his unit. The elimination of a much-feared local guerrilla leader had a tremendous effect on the morale of the villagers, and information began to flow. This, coupled with the intelligence gained from the leader himself, often resulted in an important lead into neighboring units. Special Branch might therefore keep a delicate project on ice for months, asking soldiers in ambush to hold their fire unless a particular high-ranking leader entered the target area, so that the agent would not be blown until that leader was in our hands, dead or alive.

Not every SEP was a star, however. Many were frightened

"squaddies," who had lain low for too long after their escape to leave us with any hope of reaching their camp before it moved. They could give no direct intelligence, and qualified for no spectacular rewards. They did, however, give valuable information about the personalities in their branches or platoons, and many had photographs and diaries. It was largely thanks to these SEP's that, by 1955, the great majority of guerrillas still in the jungle were listed in the district police stations, each with his photograph on a disk hanging on a nail with the rest of the gang's—until it could be tossed into the growing "dead" and "captured" boxes.

Until they could be rehabilitated and released to normal life, most SEP's were retained for months, or even years, as employees of the Special Branch. They were also used as interrogators or as informers among detainees and captured guerrillas. They provided much of the background for psychological-warfare broadcasts and leaflets, and many of the leaflets were letters from them to their ex-comrades. "Voice aircraft" droned over the gangs, broadcasting messages the SEP's had recorded on tape.

What happened to the SEP's in the end? Few had any desire to return to Communism; their mental break had been too violent for that. Many have now become affluent and respected citizens. The police keep an eye on them—and so, perhaps, do the remaining underground Communists (if they have run them to earth under their new names). So far, however, the supposedly long arm of Communist vengeance has sought few of them out. Perhaps the Communists know that, for the time being, they have more to lose by showing their hands. For their part, the SEP's seem happy and secure. Most have taken new houses and new names. One—an MCP district committee secretary who had a $12,000-reward on his head—became groundsman at the Cricket Club in the capital of the district he once terrorized. He had a sense of humor, and the Chinese will forgive a man a lot for that.

In South Vietnam, because of the consistently poor (and even self-destroying) intelligence services at village level, there are few agents; but surrenders seem to be fairly frequent. These men undoubtedly offer the most promising source of intelligence; unfortunately, there are repeated stories of Viet Cong prisoners being beaten up. This, I believe, is a tragic error. As with potential agents, so with surrendered guerrillas, torture is not the way. A surrendered Communist may know secrets of immediate value, and it is obviously tempting to extract these by torture; but this will forfeit the far greater dividend that can come from his active cooperation in interpreting enemy actions, recognizing personalities, and helping acquire information from other defectors. American advice to this effect seldom seems to be taken.[5]

There are, however, some encouraging exceptions. In the notorious Zone D, north of Saigon, neither the French nor the Vietnamese governments had been able to exercise control; in fact, it had been referred to for years in Hanoi as a liberated area. This was a pretty fair claim until the end of 1962, when a new and progressive province chief was appointed. He at once set about bringing the people to his side by visibly improving the local administration. He also launched a settlement scheme for surrendered Viet Cong; instead of being tortured, they were allotted a plot of land. Cooperation began, and operations started to succeed; as the word spread, more surrenders came in. Within four months, 250 Viet Cong had been killed and more than 100 had surrendered.

To quote the province chief's U.S. Army adviser:

The success of these operations has depended upon timely and accurate intelligence. In large measure, it has been the proper treatment of prisoners and defectors that has provided accurate information on the location of VC units in Zone D. The prisoners and defectors have been quickly won over to the government side by on-the-spot good treatment and have willingly guided Ranger columns to VC installations. . . . The operations certainly have not developed any new counterinsurgency techniques, but they have added substantial meaning to the old teaching points such as "It takes a guer-

---

[5] A correspondent of the London *Times* was present at an operation in Quang Ngai Province in March, 1965, during which a wounded Viet Cong village chief was captured. He wrote in a dispatch published March 15:

Soon afterwards there was some firing and it was understood by all that he had been shot. Elementary intelligence, if nothing else, would demand interrogation. One might also think to impress villagers that far from trying vainly to kill all the enemy, the Government treated its prisoners well in the hope of winning them over. Not so . . . the corps commander orders that all men caught with weapons be shot, and no amount of American advice can persuade the Vietnamese of their folly.

rilla to catch a guerrilla" or "Finding a guerrilla is 90 per cent of the battle."[6]

It is a vital lesson—to offer the surrendered guerrilla generous terms, and to keep faith with him. It worked for us in Malaya and for Castro in Cuba; it also seems to work for the people who have the wisdom to try it in South Vietnam.

---

[6] Major Nulsen, letter from Zone D (South Vietnam), February, 1963.

# 13

# THE ANATOMY OF
# AN OFFENSIVE OPERATION

In 1952, 1953, and 1954, our intelligence methods paid increasing dividends. Around them, we built an operational technique to which the Communists could find no answer. It was slow but thorough; once a district had been cleared, its Communist organization never revived. This must always be the test of any plan for "pacification." Five years in development, this technique was used almost without variation during the next seven years to clear the whole country of guerrillas.

Throughout this time, we maintained a framework of military pressure in all parts of the country not cleared. (These are called "economy-of-force" areas in South Vietnam.) These framework operations had to be strong enough to keep the Communist organization in check, and we had to maintain a nucleus of intelligence agents and informers on which to build.

Meanwhile, federal priority operations were mounted in selected districts, two or three at a time. These districts' troops and police were trebled or quadrupled; they operated in numerous small patrols to conduct ambushes, snap checks, etc., for several months. The aim was to damage the Communist organization so heavily, both in the jungle and in the villages, that its revival could be prevented by the district's own police and Home Guard, without any further need for the food rationing, curfews, etc., which the people had endured for so long. When this was achieved, the district was described as a white area. The first white area was declared in Malacca in 1953.

By mid-1954, the guerrillas had lost two-thirds of their strength. Their offensive capacity was so reduced that one-man rule was no longer necessary; General Templer handed over his post as High Commissioner to his civilian deputy, Sir Donald MacGillivray, and as Director of Operations to Lieutenant General Sir Geoffrey Bourne.

The situation, though vastly improved, was still dangerous. The MRLA, milked by the MCP to keep the political hierarchy and people's organizations intact over almost the whole country, was down to thirty or forty platoons; but the survivors had become hardier and better able to maintain contact with the people without exposing themselves. Their ability to withstand the government's pressure threatened to bring a stalemate—which was just what the Communists wanted, for if they lay low and kept their political and supply organization intact, the Emergency Regulations and military pressure would be relaxed, leaving the surviving guerrillas free to rebuild their offensive capacity.

General Bourne, therefore, adopted the strategy of destroying the Communist organization in the weakest areas first—that is, in the eastern and central parts of Malaya, where the Chinese population was smallest—so that these areas could all be declared white. Troops could then be concentrated on the blacker areas in the rubber and tin states astride the road and railway on the western side of the mountain spine.

Some businessmen, British and Chinese, whose profits depended on ending the war in the rubber and tin areas, opposed General Bourne's strategy. It was in these areas, they argued, that casualties and damage to the nation's economy were greatest. Surely they should have priority? These arguments were sometimes so compelling that priority operations were launched prematurely to avoid a dangerous deterioration of local morale. Such operations always proved indecisive, and none of the really black areas were finally cleared until 1958–59.

Generally, however, Bourne and his successor kept to their strategy, and this was undoubtedly right. Not only did this strategy permit them to concentrate progressively more troops and police on the blacker areas, but it made the people in these areas aware of the government successes elsewhere and of the peaceful and prosperous life to which they too could look forward when the restrictions were lifted.

Similar arguments will occur in every counterguerrilla campaign —as indeed they have in South Vietnam. The first Strategic Hamlets were set up in strong Viet Cong areas and were quickly overrun. The idea of "clear-and-hold" operations that followed this setback was discredited by the return of the Viet Cong after the troops had moved on. The more thorough and less spectacular program of pacification begun in 1965 seems much more likely to last, but only time will tell.

Figure 5 shows a typical district of the size normally selected for a federal priority operation. The district, in one of the blackest areas of Malaya, was in fact the scene of many years of framework operations interspersed with a number of priority operations that bogged down and had to be called off.

The district's rubber estates, tin mines, and tapioca plantations were worked almost entirely by Chinese and Indians. The central cultivated valley was flanked by mountainous jungle. Beyond the western mountains was another valley with a wide river, whose banks teemed with Malay kampongs; in the mountains to the east were aborigine settlements, a two- or three-day march from the central valley, that provided hiding places for the guerrillas when the pressure became too great.

Normally, only one infantry battalion was in the district, living in four company-sized camps. In each Chinese village was a police post of ten or twelve Malay constables (rising to fifty in the district capital). Supporting them was a locally recruited Home Guard of about thirty-five men in each village, five on duty each night. Most villages also had a Chinese Special Branch detective and a number

## FIGURE 5

### A Typical District

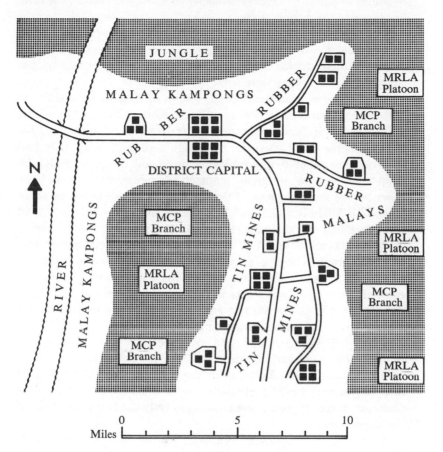

POPULATION
(only Chinese villages are shown)

53,000 Chinese in villages (  represents 1,000 Chinese)

33,000 Malays spread over areas shown

11,000 Indians (Indian villages are among the Chinese villages but are not marked)

3,000 Aborigines in jungle to the east

of Malay civilians (including women) to assist the police part time in searching the people going to work.

Rice was rationed at seven and a half pounds a week per person. It was delivered in escorted convoys, and shopkeepers had to account for their stocks. Canned foods had to be punctured by the shopkeepers when they were sold.

Curfews were strictly enforced. Everyone had to be inside the villages between dusk (6:00 P.M.) and dawn (about 6:30 A.M.), and inside their houses between 10:00 P.M. and 5:30 A.M. Although people could move on the roads until 6:00 P.M., they had to be off the plantations (rubber, tapioca, oil palm, or fruit) by 3:00 P.M. This was no great handicap for rubber tappers, as latex flows best in the early part of the day; and it gave the troops three hours of daylight in which to take up night ambush positions around the villages or in the jungle fringe. If this had been done during working hours, the patrols would have found their movements being telegraphed to the guerrillas by shouting, singing, and the clattering of tins among the rubber trees or by the waving of colored scarves by the workers in the waist-high tapioca. In a black district like this one, even the anti-Communists were afraid to let a patrol pass near them without making a signal.

Four MCP branches operated in the district, two on each side of the valley, "governing" the 53,000 Chinese villagers and organizing support for guerrillas in the district. Once the MRLA's fifth regiment, these guerrillas now formed four independent platoons; three operated from the east and one from the west of the main valley.

There was an occasional contact in which a few guerrillas were killed. There was an occasional body found in the rubber or the tapioca. There was an occasional arrest of a food smuggler at the gate. But information was scarce and surrenders were rare. It seemed reasonably quiet; but in fact, the Communists were deeply entrenched and biding their time.

The decision to mount a federal priority operation was made six months in advance. There was no noticeable reinforcement of the soldiers or police; but extra Special Branch officers moved in, and the watch for smugglers was intensified. Patrols noted suspicious movements by the people at work, and these were investigated. The Special Branch blacklists grew.

Meanwhile, jungle patrols concentrated on finding food dumps, mainly by tracking. They were assisted by dogs and by Iban (Dyak) trackers from Borneo, who could spot a broken twig or a crushed leaf and say how many men had passed that way, and how long ago. The aim at this stage was not to kill guerrillas but to reduce their reserves of food and to give the Special Branch more evidence to use against the people's organization when the time came.

Special Branch would say when they were ready for the operation proper to begin. There was then a simultaneous swoop on every village to arrest every known supplier. Police set up cordons before dawn at villages with large numbers of suspects, and all the inhabitants passed through a police screen. In this district, even in the late 1950's, such a screen sometimes caught a few suspected guerrillas having a night out of the jungle, but these were just a bonus. The aim was to break up the Communists' supply organization at a single blow, without warning. If the preceding months of intelligence buildup had been successful, as many as 500 suppliers might be arrested on the first morning of a major operation.

Now that the government had shown its hand, additional troops and police moved into the district, a brigade being superimposed on the original battalion. Patrolling was intensified, but still aimed more at gathering intelligence and cutting food stocks than at killing guerrillas. After the initial Special Branch swoop, each village in turn was again surrounded while every house was searched meticulously for hidden food or other incriminating evidence. At the same time, a few of the arrested suppliers might already have been persuaded to cooperate; they would watch through slits in truck canopies and point out other suppliers as the villagers passed through a police check beside them. Though this was a disagreeable process because some of the "cooperators" used it to settle old scores, it did yield many identifications that could be confirmed by detailed police investigation.

The rice ration was cut to five pounds a week, tight enough to mean real hunger for those who tried to save some for the guerrillas. In many villages, compulsory central cooking of rice was instituted; families collected their portions, hot and wet, from the central kitchens before each meal, adding their own bits of meat, fish, and vegetables. Since cooked rice goes bad in twenty-four hours in the Malayan climate, it could not be stored up for the guerrillas.

The people could buy as much as they liked; so, after initial opposition, central cooking became quite popular.

What was the effect of this initial effort? Suddenly, the guerrillas found themselves short of food and supporters. Most of their reserve dumps were gone, and the people in the rubber had alibis for not supplying more—strict rationing, central cooking, intensified searches at the gate, and the place swarming with patrols, they just could not oblige, much as they sympathized with the heroic . . . , etc. In addition, with most of the masses executives and trusted suppliers locked up, the organization for finding replacements had been disrupted. The surviving masses executives had to do something drastic to recruit new suppliers quickly. This was precisely what the Special Branch wanted.

Why did the MCP branches not just move elsewhere when the operation began? Some in other districts did, and their battered village organizations died; with few masses executives and no guerrillas to intimidate them, the villagers dropped out with relief. If the Communists tried later to revive the organizations, some of the villagers would be willing to act as informers rather than have the misery begin all over again. The area could be declared white without a fight. After a number of such cases, the alarmed Communist Central Committee issued strict orders that, while MRLA platoons could be mobile, the MCP branches must stay in their districts, no matter what the pressure, "serving the people" to the end.

For this reason, it was important that the priority operations encompassed all the villages in which the MCP branches had their contacts; otherwise, they would get what was needed from the outlying villages in which the organization had not been disrupted. The boundaries, in fact, had to follow Communist areas of responsibility, not government administrative boundaries, and this needed a good intelligence picture before the operation was begun.

As the federal priority operation proceeded, the 4 MCP branches in the district operated under great pressure against the government's concentrated power. Nationwide, the guerrillas were still outnumbered only 3 to 1 by infantry soldiers; but in the area of a major operation, it was more like 8 to 1. In this district, in 1955, there were about 240 guerrillas: 120 in the 4 MRLA platoons, about 40 in the district and higher committees, and 20 in each of the 4 branches. Against each branch (with its associated platoon of

30) a full infantry battalion—400 riflemen—was concentrated in the rubber and the jungle fringe, while armed police and guardsmen awaited them if they approached the perimeters of the villages.

Each branch was responsible for about 6 Chinese villages. From these, it had to get supplies into the jungle for 60 guerrillas (its own 20, a platoon of 30, and a contribution for the higher committees). Except in the aborigine areas deep in the jungle, rice could not be grown without making jungle clearings that could be spotted from the air. While the guerrillas could catch fish and game and eat some of the jungle fruits and fungi, they had to balance their diet with a cereal food or face the onset of the deadly disease of beriberi. Thus, for 60 men, the branch had to smuggle 300 pounds of rice out of 6 villages every week. The organization in some of these 6 was so shattered that the bulk of the rice came from 2 or 3 of them. In addition, the guerrillas needed salt, antimalarial drugs, aspirins, pencils and paper for propaganda, money, boots, and clothing. All this was built up into prearranged dumps near the jungle fringe, and a carrying party of guerrillas came out at least once a week to collect one of these dumps. To stock the dumps, 20 or 30 tappers had to smuggle something quite substantial through the village gates every day. With the gates well manned and the rubber well patrolled, this became quite difficult.

All the same, with 1,000 or more tappers going to work each morning, only a meticulous standard of searching could ensure that some, at least, of these 20 or 30 would be spotted. This was normally a police job; but in a major operations, the troops helped.[1] Most of the villagers queued at the gate before opening time: a sprinkling of schoolchildren, the boys in smart white shirts and shorts, waiting with satchels and bicycles to ride to the Chinese middle school in the district capital, but the vast majority tappers, each with a bicycle, a tapping knife, and a big tin bucket for the latex. Some would go out in complete families, with the older children carrying the babies, each ready to help in the work by tearing off the congealed latex ready for the next cut, or carrying the buckets of latex to the weighing shed. More than half the tap-

---

[1] For a description of troops at work on the gates and around the villages, see Richard Miers' *Shoot to Kill*.

pers were women, for in a black area like this, a noticeable proportion of the young men were in the jungle, and it was the business of the police to know which were their mothers and sisters and cousins and aunts.

Facing the lively crowd of Chinese, two impassive young Malay constables manned the gate, which could not be opened until it was light enough for the search. Some tappers, impatient to take advantage of the fact that the latex flowed faster in the cool of the day, would taunt and jeer from the safety of the crowd. Most of this jeering was reasonably good-humored, but it had an undercurrent of hostility. An over-impatient crowd, and the swing of a rifle butt by a frightened young constable could quickly lead to a riot.

In a priority operation, of course, the search was as thorough as possible. The women were searched by women in the privacy of search booths, while the men were searched in the open between sawhorses. Another team searched the bicycles, looking for false bottoms in the latex tins, packets of salt under the seat, antimalarial drugs in the bell, or rolled-up messages in the tire pump. The aim was to search the 1,000 tappers in an hour; with 8 people searching, this allowed only about 15 seconds for each tapper and bicycle. Some supplies were bound to get through; but with good supervision, smugglers were spotted, enough to give the Communists a constant headache in recruiting new ones and the police a chance to find their agents.

The search did not end here, however. During the day, a few cars or trucks and a few agricultural workers moved into or out of the villages. All had to be searched. A car could take out a day's supply of rice inside a spare tire, and a truck driver could smuggle enough for a week.

Soon after dark, the Chinese Home Guard came on duty. With rifles drawn from the police armory, they patrolled the perimeter. The dangers at night were threefold, stemming from the internal activity of the village "antitraitor squad," raids by the MRLA platoons for arms or intimidation, and the smuggling of rice sacks from supporters in the villages to branch members across the fence. If the squeeze could force them into taking such risks, of course, and the Special Branch could get wind of them, these night raids on the villages gave the best opportunities of all for an ambush.

The army patrols were active day and night. Of the battalion now attacking each MCP branch, four or five platoons usually lived in the fringes of the jungle, each for ten or twenty days at a time, listening and watching for movements or fresh tracks. Other platoons patrolled the rubber all day, checking passes and watching for anything unusual. At about 4:00 P.M., after rubber curfew, half-a-dozen ambush parties moved into position, sometimes on precise information, such as a tip about a planned guerrilla raid on a village. If there were no such information, the troops simply ambushed trails they thought the guerrillas were most likely to use. During the first few months of the operation, there were few kills. The fruits of these early patrols were hunger for the guerrillas and evidence for the Special Branch—and then the kills began to come.

# 14

# INTELLIGENCE AND THE KILLING STAGE

THE battles, even in the killing stage, were still not spectacular —nothing like the set-piece affairs in North Vietnam in the 1950's or South Vietnam in the 1960's, with whole battalions lying in ambush for each other. If we had lost the battles of 1950 and 1951, that is what our war would have been like; but we did not lose them. Although 250 guerrillas might be in the district of a major operation, we seldom met them after 1952 in parties of more than 30; most often, they numbered a dozen or less. It was rare, even at the height of the killing stage, for there to be more than six casualties in a single action. These sixes, however, built up over the weeks. A major operation was, in fact, a host of minor operations. A few typical examples are described below.[1]

---

[1] The incidents related in this chapter occurred during my time in Malaya. I have, however, changed the names of people, places, and other details; many of those concerned are still alive.

During the third month of a federal priority operation, a sharp-eyed Welsh corporal on patrol in the rubber spotted a face he had not seen before. He had been patrolling this same plantation for weeks and knew all the tappers by sight; this was not one of them. The man's pass seemed in order, but the corporal noted its number and reported it.

The police were interested; the pass number belonged to a man who was in the hospital. The Special Branch sent a Chinese detective from the village to join the corporal on his patrol. After two days, the corporal saw the man again. The detective, lying low, recognized him at once. He was not a rubber tapper at all; he was a garage mechanic.

The watch now switched to the village gate. Next time the mechanic came out, his bicycle was wheeled out of sight and carefully searched. Concealed in the frame were two flashlight batteries and six pencils. They were photographed quickly and replaced. The man suspected nothing.

Over the next month, further evidence was built up. Patrols were asked by the Special Branch to keep out of the rubber area where the mechanic had been seen. The police had no wish to scare him off, or to keep the guerrillas from contacting him; they were content to find out later where he was meeting them or dumping the supplies.

When they had all they needed, the Special Branch police waylaid him one night in the village and confronted him with the evidence. Trembling with fright, he admitted he was dumping supplies but pleaded that he had no option. He said the guerrillas gave him a "shopping list," mainly of hardware, clothing, and medicines, and warned him to have it ready by the end of the month. They would collect it when they wished. He was fairly sure, however, that they would come at night; they were afraid of the daytime patrols in the rubber. He had never met the guerrillas but had been shown by a tapper where to dump the supplies. He agreed, after some persuasion, to allow an army officer and a Special Branch man to follow him to the dump the next day; but he begged that they dress as tappers and come after rubber curfew.

The dump was well chosen. It was in a small patch of abandoned rubber, where the trees had been bled to death by slashing. The *blukar* (undergrowth) had grown ten feet high. Around this patch, the plantation was well tended, the undergrowth kept short; by night, the guerrillas could approach the patch from any direction. To put a cordon there tight enough for a night ambush would have required so many troops that they would have had little hope of maintaining it for several nights without leaving signs of occupation that would be spotted in the daytime. An ambush in the *blukar* itself was out of the question. There was no field of fire; and, unless the guerrillas came on the first night, the signs of occupation would be unmistakable.

The battalion, however, knew this area well from their many months of patrolling. They knew that along the jungle fringe, less than half a mile from the dump, there was a long stretch of marsh ground, about fifty yards wide and clear of trees. Only two paths, both disused, crossed this marsh; they were made of logs and branches thrown down by forestry workers before the war. Although it was possible to flounder across the marsh between these paths, waist deep in mud, the battalion commander could not imagine the guerrillas trying this at night. He decided to ambush the two crossings every night until something happened.

After rubber curfew, the soldiers hung waterproof flares in the trees at either end of the paths. For three nights, eight of the best shots in the battalion lay there in the marsh, coming out again before the tappers got to work. On the fourth night, the soldiers heard footsteps. Picking his time carefully, the officer touched the electric switch to ignite the flares. There, strung out along the path, were five guerrillas. The soldiers shot well (none too easy at night, when the sights of the gun cannot be seen), and they killed four.

That particular MCP branch was already seriously weakened, and it never recovered. The villages "served" by it had no more approaches from the guerrillas, and the whole district was declared a white area six months later.

The same Special Branch produced another agent for the same battalion. This was in an area where the guerrillas were bolder. They had approached a girl rubber tapper at her work and told her she was to have sixty pounds of rice dumped ready for them to collect before the Chinese New Year. They would contact her again and she would lead them to the dump.

The girl buried a huge glass jar, the kind used in industry for acid or distilled water, beside a track through a patch of rubber, with enough undergrowth to enable her to get at it without being seen from afar. Only the neck of the jar protuded from the ground among the foliage. Into this neck, almost every day, she poured a few ounces of rice, which she had smuggled out in her brassière, sewn into secret pockets in her clothes, or hidden in her bicycle pump. The quantities were small, and she varied her methods; but she was spotted, all the same.

She broke down under questioning, and attracted by the reward, which amounted to more than 20,000 Malayan dollars (U.S. $6,666), she agreed to continue to fill the jar, not to "notice" the ambush, and to lead the guerrillas into it when they came.

Ten days before the Chinese New Year, the ambush was mounted—all day, every day. Each night a fresh ambush party took up its position, the main fire section covering the jar from across the track, with cut-off parties on the next bend each way and a tracking party ready with a dog and a tracker to go off in pursuit of any guerrillas who dived into the undergrowth and got away.

The soldiers lay in the undergrowth seven yards from the track. The undergrowth was only eighteen inches high, and every day an aged tapper used to tap a tree just three yards from one of the soldiers. He never spotted them. The track was used by several other tappers during the day. The soldiers had to lie there, quiet and still, for thirteen hours on end. Their only food was an occasional nibble of raisins from their pockets; they had nothing to drink. Bodily functions had to be performed right there. It was a rare test of discipline and training. Not until dusk would the party move out; in spite of the rubber curfew, the soldiers preferred not to risk giving the game away by moving in daylight. Before dawn, the relief party would be in position. Each party was half a platoon, and each rested one day and lay in ambush the next. They kept it up for ten days.

On most days, the girl came in to empty her contribution into the mouth of the jar. It was an eerie moment. She seemed not to see the soldiers—and perhaps she never did. The strain, however, began to tell on her. The idea of walking into the ambush with the guerrillas and throwing herself flat in the crossfire became less and less attractive, even for a $20,000 reward. But there was a worse worry: Suppose a soldier *did* cough just before she and the guerrillas reached the jar? They would dive into the jungle *with her*. And then what?

She found a simple solution. She never let anyone know she was a police agent, and she never uttered a word about the dump. All she did was to remark, within earshot of a man she knew was a supplier, that the soldiers seemed particularly active in the rubber lot where she worked. She knew this would get back to the guerrillas, for this man knew she was a supplier and would deduce (rightly) that she had been spotted. That would be enough.

It was. The guerrillas never came, and the police soon had other reasons to know that they never would. The dump was destroyed and the operation called off—one of the countless ambushes that failed. Despite the failure, it illustrates two things: First, to have a hope of success in an ambush, the troops needed tremendous self-discipline and morale; secondly, agents worked under intense strain that sometimes was too much to endure, even for $20,000.

The girl with the rice jar could have done worse. She could have led our troops into an ambush and then joined the guerrillas, and this sometimes happened. Double agents are tricky fish to play.

The Kuala Lallang branch of the MCP was tough. The village of Kuala Lallang had lived in terror of it for seven years. At first, it had been twenty strong, supporting a powerful MRLA regiment. At the time of this story, a federal priority operation had been in progress for six months. The regiment, now reduced to an independent platoon, had been switched to a safer district. The branch was down to five members, four men and a girl.

Everyone in the village knew these five by sight. They were local people, and their photographs were displayed on "Wanted" notices offering huge rewards. But the people did not dare give any information. The Special Branch had no agent in the village.

At last, however, it found one; and his story, when he broke down, called for rapid action. The guerrillas were to come into the village the next night, at a point near his outside toilet where he was to loosen the barbed-wire fence, to collect five packs of food, each weighing eighty pounds.

The agent was instructed to loosen the wire as planned, and a platoon of Gurkha soldiers mounted an ambush in his tapioca patch beside the privy. It was a clear night, and the soldiers killed all five guerrillas—but not before the guerrillas had fired about fifty bullets, which cracked through the wooden walls of the houses in the village. Luckily, none of the villagers was hit.

When the firing died, there was not a sound. No one ventured out of the houses. The police went knocking; from every bed came purposeful snoring.

"What do you want, waking me up? No, I heard nothing."

"Holes in the wall? Splinters on the floor? I can't see anything."

In Kuala Lallang, it was safer to hear nothing, see nothing, and know nothing.

Next morning, the five bodies were laid outside the police station, the "Wanted" photographs beside them. Every tapper filed past while waiting to go out to work. Some of their faces made a fascinating study as they checked and rechecked—one, two, three four, *FIVE*.

That evening, the Special Branch detectives had a field day. As they went around the houses, their only worry was writer's cramp. They gathered up the names of all the principal Communist executives in the village, who were duly arrested. The news spread, and the neighboring villages followed suit. A few weeks later, the whole district was declared a white area.

The Kuala Lallang branch was high-priced. Three of the five were ranking Communists, and the agent netted 36,000 Malayan dollars (U.S. $12,000) for his night's work. Such rewards for those who had cooperated with the enemy were much criticized on moral grounds, but the benefits were worth every dollar. Compared with the cost of maintaining a battalion of infantry, a flight of helicopters, and 400 policemen in the district, $12,000 was very little. If rewards of only a few hundred dollars had been offered, would agents have been prepared to risk their lives?

Overnight, that agent in Kuala Lallang crippled the whole of the local Communist organization—for good. The head of the octopus (Figure 4) had been cut off. The people were able to do all the things they so long to do—simple things like taking a box lunch out to work and spending an evening with friends. The war was over for Kuala Lallang, and I don't think the people worried too much about who had been paid to bring this about.

Batu Bintang, a natural eminence set in a vast stretch of wet paddy flanked by miles of swampy jungle, was the scene of a major operation in miniature. The ground was so marshy that there were no other villages; all the paddy workers and vegetable growers lived in Batu Bintang. In the jungle lived the Batu Bintang MCP branch, fourteen strong, as resilient and aggressive as the branch in Kuala Lallang, and led by one of the toughest characters we knew, Kwok Lung. Kwok Lung was not popular, but he was so greatly feared by the people in the village that no one dared give information to the police.

A girl in the Batu Bintang branch had a baby. A baby's cries could give away the location of a guerrilla camp, so babies usually were smuggled out of the jungle to friends or relatives. But Kwok Lung did not want to risk this. If he let the baby out, the mother might follow; and she might be induced to talk. So he killed the baby.

The villagers learned of this, and their hatred for Kwok Lung grew; but so did their fear, and still no one came forward with information.

The local Special Branch officer knew that the villagers were not far from the breaking point. Maybe a crack of the whip would tip the scale.

Extra police came to Batu Bintang. They stringently enforced the Emergency Regulations. A strong cordon of troops hemmed in the village. A strict curfew was imposed. The villagers could go to work in the fields only after queuing for a permit and arranging for a personal escort. They often had to wait for an escort to be free. They saw their output dwindling, their wages falling. They asked how long this would go on and were told: "Until Kwok Lung and his gang are wiped out."

The cordon and the escorts prevented contact between the people and Kwok Lung, so he could no longer get food from them. Only a few dedicated Communist supporters braved the night patrols to keep in touch. Kwok Lung told these diehards to get food from the other villagers and smuggle it out. But the other villagers, who by then had had enough, denounced some of the supporters to the police, bringing the first arrests at Batu Bintang for a long time. For Kwok Lung's gang, this was very discouraging.

Meanwhile, transport aircraft, on a flight plan that had deliber-

ately been much used in recent weeks by other aircraft to allay
suspicion, dropped sixty parachutists into the jungle. They immediately split up into small patrols.

The marsh virtually restricted movement to the trails, both for
Kwok Lung and for the government forces. There was little hope
of catching a skilled guerrilla in such country; but constantly
flushed from his camp, he spent many miserable nights in the
swamp. Each time he abandoned one of his camps, he had to
leave food behind. When he went to replenish from his hidden
dumps, built up over the years, he usually found that the parachutists had destroyed them.

Kwok Lung's men were hungry, and nothing was coming from
the village but discouragement. After only ten days, the first two
surrendered, pale, bedraggled, exhausted, and fed up with Kwok
Lung. Information they gave was flashed to the parachutists, and
the chase became hotter. Three more surrendered. Then the parachutists killed two, and two more terrified guerrillas scuttled out
of the swamp. Kwok Lung was left with only four diehards—with
whom he finally surrendered, less than a month after the operation
had begun.

Kwok Lung was paraded before the people of Batu Bintang,
all restrictions were lifted, and Batu Bintang became a white area.
For the villagers, the agony was over.

Not every operation ended as tidily as those at Kuala Lallang
and Batu Bintang. Usually, as the guerrilla strength ebbed, the
kills would decline; and the Special Branch would have to judge
whether the Communist organization was broken beyond recovery.
Probably all they knew for certain was that the MRLA platoons
had withdrawn to lighten the food load on the MCP branches under
attack. The MCP branch, reduced to perhaps five or six men,
would now have only itself to feed; and it was not so difficult to
smuggle twenty to thirty pounds of rice a week from six villages.
If all the Special Branch agents had either lost their usefulness or
were no longer in touch with the guerrillas, there might be little
hope of getting more agents, because the guerrilla contacts with
the people were so few. Even for a whole battalion, thrashing the
jungle in search of five men became a fruitless task if there was
no information. This left two alternatives: to call the priority opera-

tion off and revert to framework operations, or to take a calculated risk and declare a white area.

Calling off the operation was a hard decision to make. The Special Branch well knew that as soon as the pressure was relaxed, the MCP branches might be brought up to fifteen or twenty men again; and then the platoons, even though reduced in numbers, would come back into the area. The inhabitants, so ready to cooperate during the killing stage, now would be disillusioned. It would be far more difficult to get their cooperation next time. Meanwhile, any undetected masses executives would get to work on recruiting more guerrillas, rebuilding the village organization, and taking revenge on government collaborators.

Such decisions, however, had to be made. There were enough troops for only three or four federal priority operations at a time. There were some sixty MCP districts to be dealt with. Once an operation had bogged down, with no intelligence or prospect of intelligence, these troops would be better employed if they were switched to a fresh district.

A federal priority operation usually ended, one way or the other, after about twelve months. By that time, either the district was ready, or nearly ready, to be declared a white area, or the operation clearly had bogged down. Sometimes, a compromise solution would be to leave a reinforced framework operation, strong enough to finish the job while the bulk of the troops moved off to the next district on the list. This often succeeded, and within six more months the district was declared white.

Generally, until 1957, the federal priority operations in the eastern half of the country led to white areas at, or soon after, their conclusion; but the districts astride the main road through the rubber and the tin needed two or more priority operations. The blackest areas in Perak and Johore needed three or four.

Pressure was usually strong on the Special Branch to declare an area white before it was ready. This pressure came both from politicians and from the local government of the district itself, who argued that if the restrictions were lifted, the people would respond by giving information voluntarily. The Special Branch would maintain, however, that once the curfews, food rationing, and gate checks were relaxed, the guerrillas would be able to get all they needed from a handful of absolutely reliable supporters without taking any risks. The ordinary people would have no contact with them and therefore no information. The war would be back to the 1950 stage, and the MCP district organization would begin to grow again.

The Special Branch usually won this argument, and it is a fact that no white area ever reverted to black—the people always saw to it that the organization did not revive. While in Malaya, I was always on the side of the Special Branch in being cautious about lifting the restrictions; but in retrospect, I believe that we may have been too cautious—100 per cent right is almost too good to be true, and I now think that some bolder gambles might have been regarded by the people as a sign of confidence and might have ended the war a year or two sooner. This, however, is easy to say now. It looked very different to the Special Branch officers, worrying over their secret files, uncomfortably aware that there were undetected Communists not in the files at all, and reluctant to abandon the villagers who had helped them. If these men were overcautious, their defense is that they knew more than the rest of us, that this was essentially a Special Branch war, and that they did win it.

# THREE

# VICTORY (1955-60)— AND THEN WHAT?

# 15

## THE WAY TO INDEPENDENCE

CHIN PENG decided to make overtures of peace in 1955, mainly because he knew he was losing. There was, however, a second reason: the achievement of Malayan self-government and the imminence of complete independence had knocked the bottom out of his "liberation" movement. This was obvious from the dwindling enthusiasm of the villagers to risk their lives for the movement. Violence had clearly failed, so it was time for another change in tactics. In June, 1955, just before the first elections under the new constitution, he inspired (by roundabout means) a letter from a third party that indicated he would discuss a political solution.

This was fully in accordance with Communist principle and Communist history. The strong British Colonial Government was about to be replaced by a newly elected "bourgeois" government. Like all such governments it should be weak and liberal—a nice fat bunny.

In December, 1955, complex negotiations brought Chin Peng to a prearranged clearing on the fringe of the jungle near the border of Thailand. He was met there by another lone figure, John Davis, who had been with him in the jungle in 1943–45. Davis conducted him to the nearby village of Baling, and left him there. The negotiations were conducted entirely by Malayans, led by the newly elected Chief Minister of the Federation, Tunku Abdul Rahman.

Both sides badly wanted to end the war, Chin Peng because he was losing it, the Malayans because it would enable their first years of government to be years of unburdened economic expansion.

The government's terms were generous. To any surrendered guerrillas who proved themselves willing to abandon Communist activities and to be loyal, the government offered an amnesty and help in re-establishing themselves in their normal position in society. Those refusing to give up Communism would be kept in detention or, if they preferred, repatriated to China.

The negotiations were unexpectedly cordial. Chin Peng made a friendly start and pledged his full support to the Tunku's administration in completing the advance from self-government to full independence. He was willing to disband his army, but only if the Communists were free to operate as a legal political party in the new Federation. Many "emerging" politicians have given in to this kind of proposal, but Tunku Abdul Rahman would not; he had seen what the Communists did as a legal party in Malaya in 1945–48 and knew that, even if they played along until the last vestige of British power had gone, they would then resume their campaign of political infiltration, subversion, strikes, riots—whatever was needed, violent or otherwise, to seize power.

The Tunku could have played a trick out of the Communist handbook; he could have agreed to make the Communist Party legal, to release the detainees (each one carefully shadowed) and thereby lured the guerrillas out of the jungle to hand in their arms; then he could pick on some pretext to declare the Party illegal and arrest them all again. He was, however, a big enough man to know that this kind of thing rebounds.

The Tunku was certainly honest in these negotiations, but so, up to a point, was Chin Peng. He, too, could have agreed to "renounce" Communism, on his own and on his supporters' behalf, he could have bided his time, weakening the new government until the time was ripe to act. This would have been a perfectly legitimate Communist means to achieve the end. But Chin Peng openly admitted that his aim was to convert Malaya to Communism. His insistence on recognition for the Communist Party was, however, more than mere idealism. Recognition would have enabled him to claim afterward that it was really the Communists who had fought and won the fight for independence, as his propaganda had always claimed. On the other hand its extinction—even if followed later by clandestine revival—would have killed this claim forever, and he realized that he would be fatally discredited in the eyes of the people. While he was prepared to agree to almost everything else, therefore, he stuck out for recognition of the Party, and when he saw that he could not get this, he returned to the jungle to face a future of hardship and hopeless warfare, while the Malayan ministers returned to Kuala Lumpur, knowing that their first years of power must continue to be plagued by guerrilla warfare, and by the unpopular restrictions that go with it.

In a strange way, the breakdown reflected credit on both sides. The strength of character of the idealistic Communist (and Chin Peng is certainly that) needs no stressing, but few democratic politicians would have shown such confidence as Tunku Abdul Rahman so soon after coming to power—but then, few leaders come to power with fifty-one out of fifty-two seats in their first election.

From 1955 to this day, Malaya's strength has come from her stable government. The evolution of this government, and in particular the way in which Tunku Abdul Rahman welded the rival racial parties into one, is a model of its kind, and provides some of the most important lessons of the war.

The imposition of the Malayan Union in 1946[1] had caused a bitter reaction among the Malay people, and part of this reaction was the formation of the United Malay National Organization (UMNO), led by Dato Onn bin Jaafar. During the next two years, the British gave independence to India, Pakistan, Ceylon, and Burma; this increased the desire of the Malays for the independence of Malaya, though at this stage they visualized their independence

---

[1] See Chapter 2.

in terms of the nine Malay states under their own Sultans.[2] In 1948, the British Government abandoned the idea of the Malayan Union, and the Federation of Malaya was born, incorporating the nine Malay states and the two British settlements of Penang and Malacca, but excluding Singapore with its predominantly Chinese population. The federal constitution restored much of the power to the Sultans and their state governments; it specifically declared the British Government's intention to establish self-government. Citizenship rights were extended to enable Chinese and Indian immigrants who had spent fifteen of the previous twenty years in Malaya to apply for full citizenship.

In February, 1949, the Malayan Chinese Association (MCA) was formed by Tan Cheng Lok, a Chinese whose family had been in Malaya for many generations. Its aims were to promote better citizenship rights for the Malayan Chinese and to attract the poorer Chinese away from the Communist Party. Sponsored and supported mainly by the rich Chinese *towkays* (businessmen), the MCA initially was regarded with some reserve by the squatters and villagers. But the *towkays* raised a huge sum of money ($2.5 million) by means of lotteries to help the poor Chinese, and over the next few years, the MCA gained ground both in the cities and in the rural areas.

Meanwhile, the Indians had also formed a political party, the Malayan Indian Congress (MIC).

Thus, prompted by the ill-starred Malayan Union, the people of Malaya had by 1949 formed political parties on the worst possible basis—by race.

The danger of this racial organization was appreciated by almost all the communal leaders, who opened their membership to the other races. The response, however, was poor; the Malays, Chinese, and Indians stuck to the parties of their own race.

In 1951, Dato Onn abandoned UMNO and set up a multiracial party, the Independence of Malaya Party (IMP). It was then that Tunku Abdul Rahman entered the political scene, taking over UMNO from Dato Onn at the age of forty-eight. Born in 1903, the fifth son of the Sultan of Kedah (with a Siamese mother), he

---

[2] The nine Malay states were Johore, Negri Sembilan, Salangor, Pahang, Perak, Kedah, Perlis, Kelantan, and Trengganu.

had graduated in law at Cambridge in the 1920's. Popular and easygoing, caring more for sports than for serious work, he had failed his bar finals in 1931. After a period in the Kedah civil service, he had worked with Dato Onn in forming UMNO in 1946 and then returned to Britain to complete his bar finals in 1949.

When the Tunku took over UMNO, the British Government had begun preparing the country for independence on the model successfully developed in India between the wars: gradually bringing elected members into the federal executive and legislative councils, and at the same time introducing fully elected municipal and village councils.

It was at these municipal elections in Kuala Lumpur in February, 1952, that UMNO and MCA brought about a most unexpected and (as it proved) far-reaching electoral pact. This, the birth of the Alliance Party, was initially an alliance against IMP and Dato Onn, whom the leaders of both parties distrusted. By agreeing not to field candidates against each other, UMNO and MCA between them won nine of the eleven seats on the Kuala Lumpur Municipal Council.

From this moment, IMP withered away and the Alliance Party, now joined by the MIC, grew. In 1954, Dato Onn abandoned the IMP and formed the Negara Party. This was a political reversal, since his aim in this party was to attract the Malay vote away from the now multiracial Alliance; but this proved an even more dismal failure than IMP. It was now clear to the British that the political leaders with whom to negotiate independence were Tunku Abdul Rahman and Tan Cheng Lok.

It takes at least thirty years to prepare a colony for independence from the time that there is a serious intention to do so. This is the time that it takes to put a generation through school, select enough of the best for university training, and give the graduates practice in their professions before they take up the leadership. The British had been working for this in Malaya since the 1920's and 1930's, i.e., thirty years before 1957. Though the Japanese forced a break from 1942 to 1945, this had little effect, since most of the future leaders had already been through a university (like Tunku Abdul Rahman) or were halfway through and able to resume after the war (like Deputy Premier Tun Abdul Razak). The majority of these graduates, of course, were not politicians, but civil servants, lawyers, doctors, engineers, teachers, etc.—the great educated middle class without which no political leader can run a modern state.

Thirty years, however, is far too long for leaders of spirit to wait. They want independence in time for the country to be governed by them, not by their sons. Indeed, many leaders of newly independent Commonwealth countries had pressed their impatience to the extent of imprisonment or detention.

Tunku Abdul Rahman never went to prison, partly because he himself is an exceptionally tolerant man, but also because things moved fast enough after 1947 to keep well ahead of the breaking point.

As in other emerging colonies and protectorates, the British introduced local members into both the Federal Executive Council (equivalent to the Cabinet) and the Legislative Council in 1948. The intention was to increase these until, in ten years or so, there would be a majority of elected over nominated members. At this stage, the country would be self-governing, though the British High Commissioner would retain a veto and the power if necessary to suspend the constitution.

During the self-government stage, the British-nominated members would gradually be replaced by local members until, on Independence Day, the last British members and the High Commissioner would withdraw, leaving the country a running concern.

This political process cannot really begin until about twenty of the thirty years have elapsed; that is, until there are local politicians and administrators of sufficient education and experience to take executive responsibility (albeit initially shared with British colleagues). The remaning ten years are split into the period of legislative minority (1948–55 in Malaya) and the period of self-government by an elected majority (1955–57). Even the minority stage is very important; the leaders not only gain experience of responsibility, but also see the problems of government in terms of "we" instead of "they." Under a colonial administration in which they have no responsible part, the local leaders acquire the habit of being wholly obstructive. They can blame all wrongs on the colonial government. As a member of the Executive, however, each finds himself personally responsible for schools, postal services, rural development, or road construction; and, as a member of the Legislative Council, he has to vote for taxation to raise the money, knowing that no money means no schools or no roads. A few years of this responsibility can alter his whole outlook on running his country.

A typical life history is that of Tun Abdul Razak, who entered the University of Malaya (then called Raffles College) in 1940, completed his education at Cambridge after the war, practiced law from 1949 to 1951, and entered the Legislative Council in 1951. He then served for a time as chief minister of a state before becoming Minister of Education for the self-government stage in 1955 and Minister of Defense and Deputy Prime Minister in the first fully independent government in 1957.

Of course, the Tunku and the Alliance Party wanted to go faster than the British thought wise. On purely administrative grounds, the case for a slower pace was unanswerable; but human considerations outweighed them. Just as President Quezon said he would "rather be governed like hell by Filipinos than like heaven by Americans,"[3] so the Tunku said he would rather have bad self-government than good colonial government. This is fine, so long as it is not carried too far, as happened in the Congo, with disastrous results for the ordinary people.[4] The answer, of course, was a compromise.

In 1953, the Alliance Party demanded an elected majority of three to two in the Legislative Council and independence within three years. In 1954, Templer, overriding the advice of a cautious all-party committee, announced that elections would be held in 1955 for a new Legislative Council that would have fifty-two elected members and forty-six nominated members. Though this majority was still too small to satisfy the impatient members of the Alliance Party, it worked to the party's advantage in an odd way.

Local political leaders assumed, wrongly but understandably, that the forty-six nominated members would "oppose" the parties

---

[3] Lennox A. Mills, *Malaya—A Political and Economic Appraisal,* p. 88.
[4] "Many UN teams visiting bush villages in the Congo have been asked the pathetic question 'When will this Independence end? When will we see the good life again?' I do not understand politics, but I believe that if world opinion insists that politicians of under-developed countries must be given the right to be wrong, then the world should know what happens to the rest of the 'free' population." Lawson, *Strange Soldiering.*

fighting for *merdeka* (freedom). If, therefore, the fifty-two elected members were split between rival parties, they would constantly be frustrated; if, however, they formed a solid bloc they would have things their own way, subject only to the High Commissioner's veto, which they knew would seldom, if ever, be used.

Unity, therefore, was the campaign theme of the Alliance Party. Its opponents were Dato Onn's Negara Party and the Pan-Malayan Islamic Party (PMIP), both appealing mainly to the Malay or Moslem vote. The Tunku firmly overruled UMNO objections against running large numbers of Chinese and Indian Alliance candidates in predominantly Malay constituencies, and these candidates triumphed. Every Negara candidate (including Dato Onn himself) was defeated, and only one PMIP candidate was elected. The other fifty-one seats went to the Alliance Party. A great danger facing Malaya, racial party alignment, was removed.

The party and racial structure of the 1955 Legislative Council included:

| | Malays | Chinese | Indians | Eurasians | British | Total |
|---|---|---|---|---|---|---|
| Alliance Party | 34 | 15 | 2 | – | – | 51 |
| PMIP | 1 | – | – | – | – | 1 |
| Nominated | 15 | 11 | 7 | 1 | 12 | 46 |
| TOTAL | 50 | 26 | 9 | 1 | 12 | 98 |

The nominated members were not, in fact, an "opposition." They were selected by the state governments, the chambers of commerce, the mining and rubber-planting associations, and the trade unions, which presented their selections to the High Commissioner; in every case, he accepted and nominated them. Only twelve of the forty-six were British; and, even if they had voted against the government (which they did not), the Alliance could rely on a large majority. It was this support, coupled with his huge popular vote, that sustained the Tunku as Chief Minister in his firm stand at the truce talks with Chin Peng, five months after the election.

The Executive Council was made up of ten elected ministers (all members of the Legislative Council) and five nominated members. The High Commissioner was bound to carry out Executive Council decisions; he could refer any disagreement, jointly with the Chief Minister, to the British Government, which retained the final power of veto until Independence Day. This veto was never used, but its existence provided a desirable brake to discourage wild ideas.

Early in 1956, his prestige high after the truce talks, Tunku Abdul Rahman went to London to negotiate final independence. The British Government agreed to fix August 31, 1957, as Independence Day. In the happiest of celebrations, to which the Tunku invited General Templer back as an honored personal guest, power was handed over, and Sir Donald MacGillivray took off for England. The new flag bore an intentional resemblance to the Stars and Stripes, with a yellow crescent and star on blue ground in the top left quarter and eleven red-and-white bars filling the other three quarters, to represent the eleven states of the Federation.

# 16

## FOREIGNERS IN AN INDEPENDENT COUNTRY

MERDEKA DAY—August 31, 1957—was Tunku Abdul Rahman's day, and all but the Communists rejoiced with him in his triumph. He was, however, both modest and realistic; he knew well that political independence alone was not enough. It must be backed by a professional hierarchy of administrators, executives, and officials without which no country can be viable in the modern world, least of all a country like Malaya, which must live by trade. More than 40 per cent of Malaya's gross national product goes into the exports on which the people depend for their standard of living. Malayans have a per capita income nearly three times as high as that of their Indonesian neighbors, who have similar natural resources but lack Malaya's organization to exploit them.

Tunku Abdul Rahman, like President Sukarno, had many problems. Malaya's industry and agriculture needed to be developed. The nation's economy was too vulnerable to fluctuations in the price of rubber and tin. As her population was growing at 3 per cent a year, her economy had to grow at more than this rate; this required not only foreign capital but an expanding communications system. The rural Malays were generally poorer than the Chinese, and the widening gap would cause unrest unless there was a healthy program of rural development. Malaya's public administration was efficient and not corrupt, but needed to be kept that way as the British officials moved out. Still faced with a Communist insurgency and liable to threats from powerful neighbors, Malaya needed to strengthen her police and armed forces and to arrange mutual defense treaties. Above all, she had to educate more and more of her own people to carry out these tasks.

It does not take long to train craftsmen and clerks, and there is no shortage of labor in Asia. Nor is there any shortage of contestants for the relatively small number of top-level posts in the executive and legislative bodies. The problem arises at the middle levels, where jobs must be measured in thousands:

*Industry and agriculture:* scientists, engineers, managers, technicians;

*Economy and trade:* economists, bankers, merchants, transport and communications experts;

*Public administration:* civil servants, lawyers, doctors, engineers;

*Internal and external defense:* police officers, army officers;

*Education and training:* teachers, instructors, professors.

The need to train these people is the very real factor that makes it impossible to bring an undeveloped country to viable independence in less than thirty years. This training must go on parallel with the political development described in the previous chapter. Even thirty years, however, is never quite enough time to complete the task; indeed, by the time even half the number required have been trained and established in office, the pressure for independence by the political leaders will be irresistible. As in India, Pakistan, and Ghana, and as later in the other African colonies, the British gave in to this pressure with a good grace, early enough to retain the good will that was necessary if British individuals were to stay on while the balance of the Malayans were trained to replace them.

It worked. Despite grim forecasts from outside the country of chaos and communal riots when British control was lifted, Merdeka

Day came and went without a trace of racial tension or of hostility to the British. I lived in Kuala Lumpur with my family at the time, and we can all testify to this. My wife was teaching in a multiracial school with Malay, Chinese, Indian, and British children in her class. Our two sons were the only white children in a Sunday school run by two Christian college girls who between them shared Indonesian, Chinese, Indian, and English blood. The Merdeka celebrations themselves—the lights, the decorations, the music, and the flag ceremony—were run by a British member of the Malayan civil service. He and I were among the thousands of British people who stayed on as employees of the new Malayan Government. They paid us more than the British and charged us less income tax. They wanted us to stay.

At the Tunku's request, every Malayan minister had at least one senior British civil servant on his staff. The Malayan Defense Minister also had a British Director of Operations and another British general commanding the Federation Army. Most of the senior army and police officers were still British, and so were many of the senior doctors, lawyers, and engineers. We were there only for so long as they chose to pay us. We were all responsible to elected Malayan ministers, with no channel at all, either open or secret, to London. We did not want one.

Above all, we were employees, not advisers. We worked as executives, taking orders and giving orders without regard to our race or color. I am convinced that this is not only more efficient, but also more psychologically acceptable to a newly emerging nation. Here, I believe, we had a great advantage over U.S. soldiers and officials serving as advisers in South Vietnam.

The war continued unabated after Independence Day. Less than half the troops were Malayan, the remainder being from Britain and other Commonwealth countries. They were organized in two divisions:

| *Federation Division* | *Commonwealth Division* |
|---|---|
| 3  brigade headquarters | 4  brigade headquarters |
| 8  battalions | 13  battalions (5 British, 6 Gurkha, 1 Australian, 1 New Zealand) |

Both divisional commanders were members of the Emergency Operations Council (EOC) under the chairmanship of the Prime Minister or Defense Minister, whose executive officer was the Director of Operations.

Brigade commanders were members of the State War Executive Committees. In one state (Perak) there were a Federation *and* a Commonwealth brigade, so *both* brigade commanders were members of the Perak SWEC. In other states, the troops were all either Federation or Commonwealth, so there was only one kind of brigade commander on the SWEC, commanding the same kind of troops with the same kind of battalion commander on the District War Executive Committees.

The Malayan troops and Commonwealth troops were thus under separate command, although their operational direction came from the Malayan Government, through the Malayan chairmen of SWEC's and DWEC's.

There was an important saving clause over the employment of British and other non-Malayan troops. If the commander of a British battalion had ever been asked by his Malayan DWEC chairman to carry out tasks that did not accord with British Government policy or British public opinion (e.g., if he had been asked to open fire on an inhabited village), he had the right of appeal to his British brigade commander on the SWEC. If the brigade commander could not persuade his SWEC to overrule the DWEC order, then he in turn had the right of appeal to his Commonwealth divisional commander on the EOC, who could veto the order on behalf of the British (or Australian or New Zealand) Government. The knowledge that this clause existed meant that it never had to be used, but some such power of veto is an essential safeguard for troops employed under foreign direction.[1]

The relationship between British troops and Malayan villagers suffered no change at all after Independence Day. The soldiers were still based in camps outside the village perimeters, and they

---

[1] An identical veto system was used in all Commonwealth Forces in World War II. It was in fact invoked by General Freyberg on behalf of the New Zealand division in Egypt in 1942 when he was told by his British commander in chief that he must fight without having tanks under his command. Freyberg asserted his right of appeal to the New Zealand Prime Minister, who referred it to Prime Minister Churchill in London. General Freyberg got his tanks.

operated mainly in and around the jungle fringe, leaving patrolling within the village to the police and Home Guard. The Chinese, in fact, generally preferred having British troops to Malay troops in their area, since they knew the British were politically disinterested and had the reputation of getting rid of the guerrillas more quickly. I have no doubt that U.S. and Australian units operating in Vietnam are equally welcome.

Some of those who transferred to Federation employment in 1957 are there to this day, including two of the most efficient police officers I knew. They work as deputies to Malayans. While the generals and brigadiers and colonels in the army are Malayans, many of their staff members are British so that the young Malayan officers can be released to command their troops in the war with Indonesia.

As the older British officials drop out, growing numbers of younger ones come in to serve as teachers and technicians, in many cases under the VSO (Voluntary Service Overseas) scheme, which is equivalent to the U.S. Peace Corps. These young people are especially welcomed.

Meanwhile, British-owned plantations, mines, and businesses continue to operate; British capital continues to flow into the country. There seems to be no reason why this should not continue to the benefit of both sides, as it has in India, where there are now more British people living than before independence was granted.

Although the British were willing to stay for as long as the Malayans wanted them, there was an urgent effort in the last two years before Independence Day to train as many Malayans as possible to replace them, particularly in positions dealing directly with the people. By Merdeka Day, most district police officers, infantry company commanders, and middle-level civil servants were Malayans, largely as a result of a crash training program concentrated on these levels in 1955–57. A young Malayan graduating from college in 1955, for example, would first take a six-month course in local government. He would then go for a year as assistant to a British district officer in the field, proving himself and gaining the confidence of the people in the district. Then he would go back to school for a six-month advanced course before returning to take over as district officer.

Once independence had come, the Malayans continued to maintain good relations with the British officials. While they have naturally wished to Malayanize their services as quickly as possible, the Malayan leaders have struck a wise balance between political need and practical common sense.

# 17

## REMOTE AREAS AND
## THE BORDER PROBLEM

THE mountainous jungle along the central spine of Malaya is occupied by aborigine tribesmen who bear many resemblances to the *montagnards* in Vietnam. Until 1952, the government let these aborigines live their own lives, interfering only if they failed to observe some forestry or fishing regulation on the outskirts of the main populated areas. But the tribesmen seldom penetrated even this far, and few people went out to see them. Even in the anti-Japanese war, the Communist guerrillas were able to live close enough to the jungle fringe to get all they needed from the Chinese squatters; they had little to do with the aborigines.

Military pressure in 1951, however, forced the guerrillas to establish deep jungle bases for their higher echelons and for training new MRLA units. Initially, they grew much of their own food; but, because rice and tapioca can be grown in the jungle only by felling the trees to let the sun come through, their cultivations were soon spotted by British aircraft and either ambushed or destroyed. The Communists, therefore, turned increasingly for food to the aborigine tribes, whose cultivations were already in being and would excite no attention.

Most of these tribes lived a seminomadic life in small groups of from twenty to a hundred, usually a three- or four-day march from the populated areas. They set up their bamboo long houses along the banks of the mountain streams, catching fish and game with blowpipes and growing dry rice and tapioca by a system known as "shifting cultivation." This consisted of felling an area of jungle and burning the dead trees and undergrowth to make ash to fertilize the soil. From this they drew only one or two crops. Then they moved on, burning their long houses behind them, to fell a fresh area of jungle farther along the river. Their abandoned cultivations soon became a dense tangle of secondary jungle. The Chinese guerrillas set about making friends with these nomadic tribes, helping them to grow more food in exchange for a share of it.

The aborigines knew nothing of politics. "Malaya" to them was a strange valley at the foot of the streams, populated by "foreign" Malays and Chinese whom they did not much like. If they had ever heard the word "government" at all, their image of it was a seemingly interfering official who may once have driven them out of some forest reserve or water catchment area. Attempts were made by the government from time to time to resettle the aborigines in villages closer to civilization, but they pined for their nomadic life; when allowed out of the village to work, they would vanish and head out again for the deep jungle.

The only possibility of holding these people lay in extending the services of government to their own ground, in such a form that they would be attracted away from the guerrillas by things the guerrillas could not give them: trade, education, and, above all, medical care.

The first stage was to find out where these small groups of aborigines lived and establish friendly contact with them. This task was given to the Special Air Services (SAS) Regiment, the nearest equivalent to the United States Special Forces. Guided initially by air reconnaissance of the aborigine clearings, SAS troop units, each about fifteen strong, went in on foot or by helicopter and lived in the jungle, based on air supply, each staying in for thirteen weeks before relief by a fresh unit.

Accompanied by members of the government's Aborigine Department, the troops made no attempt to interfere with the aborigines' movements or way of life but offered them the beginning of an outlet for trade through their helicopters and air-drop contacts. Fish, food, and bamboo poles were paid for with tools and cloth from the towns. The troop medical men were soon surrounded by a large daily "sick call," and when needed, a doctor would be brought in by helicopter. The people began to realize that these soldiers could and would do far more for them than the guerrillas, who had now scuttled away to some neighboring tribe where there were no SAS posts.

The next stage was to develop these posts into a system of jungle forts. Sites for the forts were chosen in places where there were patches of suitable ground that could later be cleared of jungle to make strips for light aircraft and reduce the calls on helicopters. Each fort housed a police garrison of about a hundred men, with a trading post, primary school, and health clinic. Many people feared that such static forts would be easy targets for big guerrilla units re-forming in the deep jungle around them, but once again it was the local people who decided. The aborigines themselves provided a screen to warn of enemy approach. They "shifted their cultivations" without any prompting to the land around the fort. It was in their interest to keep the guerrillas from disrupting their improved way of life, and many young aborigines enlisted as volunteers to patrol around the fort and deep into the jungle where the enemy might be.

Today, there is no guerrilla threat in these areas; the garrisons of the forts have shrunk to small police posts. But the schools, the health clinics, and the trading shops still operate; and the inhabitants still center around them, living the life that suits them, but with benefits they never had before.

We found that a similar approach was needed to deal with another kind of remote people who lived on the border of Thailand.

The Communists could get anything they wanted into Malaya. The simplest route was through the free port of Singapore, which has a vast turnover of entrepôt cargoes. With a strong Communist

Party among a population 75 per cent Chinese, Singapore presented little problem in smuggling men and supplies into the port and across the half-mile stretch of water that separates the island from the jungles of South Johore.

Alternatively, Malaya has more than 2,000 miles of coastline, mainly covered with jungle and shallow sandy beaches; its smooth seas teem with coasting junks and fishing boats, day and night.

Finally, there is the Thai border. Apart from three frontier posts in cultivated land, most of this border consists of dense mountainous jungle stretching for miles on either side; no one could have prevented the Communists from filtering as many men and supplies through the jungle into Malaya as they chose.

Many wild ideas were produced for clearing a swath of jungle along the border; but even nuclear clearing (if it were a practicable proposition) would have achieved nothing, since the masses of troops or police that would have been needed to guard it were far more urgently needed for the main battlegrounds around the villages. Nor was this really necessary, for the Communists preferred to get the bulk of their recruits and supplies from within the country, not only because it was easier but because they thereby "committed" people to their support.

The significance of the Thai border was that it provided an active sanctuary for Chin Peng and some 400 hard-core guerrillas whom he held as reserve units with his Central Committee. They have lived there with little interference for more than ten years. They were, and still are, able to live in large camps of a hundred or more, just as they did in the Malayan jungles in 1949. It is easy to criticize the Thai Government for this; but no Thai Government has yet been willing to introduce the necessarily stringent Emergency Regulations for the sake of a few hundred guerrillas reputedly in the deep jungle at the remotest southern end of Thailand's Kra Isthmus. The Thai rubber tappers and paddy growers have never been resettled and are largely unprotected, so they can hardly be blamed if they provide food for the guerrillas. Remote peoples in Asia have done this for local bandit gangs all their lives.

It was from this sanctuary that Chin Peng emerged for the abortive truce talks in December, 1955; thereafter, it assumed growing importance. Realizing by then that his military campaign inside Malaya was lost, he based his plans on rebuilding his influence in the Chinese villages as the Emergency Regulations were relaxed, starting with those closest to the Thai border. Since we had no means of ousting him from Thailand, we had to find a way of insulating the border.

Kedah, the northern border state of Malaya, is a rich rice-growing region. Food control, so effective elsewhere, was virtually impossible there. If Chin Peng and his surviving guerrillas could live in the jungle fringes within range of the paddy workers' villages, the foundations for a guerrilla revival would be strong. This fringe area was different from the rest of Malaya. The roads and tracks branched out and ended like fingers as they approached the wild mountainous jungle ridge that was the frontier. Many of the small valleys in the foothills were settled by a Malay-Thai breed, the Sum-Sums. They were not as primitive as the aborigines, nor as nomadic. They cultivated wet paddy in small, isolated fields beside the narrow streams. The only way these people could reach a market or a doctor was on foot along fifteen or twenty miles of jungle trail, so they had little contact with the outside world.

The Communist guerrillas were friendly with them. They helped the Sum-Sums with their cultivation and paid them for surplus rice, usually at more than market price. The arrangement suited both sides. The guerrillas were able to live in comfort within easy marching distance of their real target for subversion, the Chinese paddy growers around the fingers of road in the plains of Kedah.

As with the aborigines, the answer was for the government to provide the Sum-Sums with more of the things they wanted than the Communists could give them—security, education, medical care, and an easier market for their crops.

The solution in this case was a sixty-four-mile loop of roadway bowed out from the fingers of the existing roads, built by army engineers in 1957–58. The effect has been exactly as hoped. These remote people now have a stake in the government, which has provided improvements without destroying their traditional way of life. Doctors and teachers work among them, and a regular truck collects their produce for cash. Police posts and patrols keep them free from molestation by the Chinese guerrillas. The guerrillas themselves keep away, as they know that the Sum-Sums will tell the police if they appear. So the Communists have been driven back to the deep jungle frontier, a three- or four-day march from the only people on whom they could ever hope to base a revival—the Chinese villagers in the plains. They have now lost contact with these villagers.

Both in the Thai border area and in the aborigine areas, the problems were the same as in the remote areas of South Vietnam. People who have never tasted the benefits of government are ripe to be "governed" by the guerrillas. With our technical resources, we can and must outbid the Communists.

The army is particularly suited to this task for many reasons: The troops are armed and ready to look after themselves; they accept being shot at or blown up by mines as a legitimate hazard; they are geared to living on air supply.[1]

Infantrymen and medical men are the spearhead, supported by helicopters. They should be accompanied, or followed soon after, by army engineers, who can build light aircraft strips and roads and handle a mass of other things to relieve the people's hardships, such as irrigation, drainage, water supply, and sanitation. The sight of army engineers in uniform, using their skills and equipment directly for the benefit of the people, creates an entirely new image of the army.

The economic development of rural and remote areas is now recognized as one of the biggest factors in countering Communist subversion. To succeed, however, it must be simple and direct. The people must be able to detect unmistakable improvements in their own way of life, and to see projects going on around them that will continue to increase their own prosperity. Provided that the ordinary people's confidence in this progress is maintained, they will not wish to upset the applecart, and Communist subversion will find nothing on which to take root.

We can do these things because we have the men, the know-how, the equipment, and the organization that the guerrillas lack.

---

[1] The French found the same in Algeria. In the remote mountain settlements of Kabylia, they had 600 army doctors and 250 nurses giving nearly a million consultations a month to the tribesmen and their families, and 1,000 soldier-teachers ran schools in remote villages for 60,000 Moslem children. That was how—in General Challe's time—they achieved such massive support for France, and won a victory that the politicians and economists decided not to accept. It is doubtful whether these doctors and teachers could ever have been persuaded to work there out of uniform.

# 18

## AIR SUPPORT

Government forces in Malaya had the advantage of a monopoly of air power, as they do in Vietnam. This advantage is sometimes compared with that enjoyed by nineteenth-century European troops armed with rifles fighting natives with spears, but this is an exaggeration. Until they start operating as conventional forces, guerrillas are seldom vulnerable to air attack, and even the flexibility of air transport is often nullified by its self-advertisement contrasted with the guerrillas' invisibility. Air support, both offensive and transport, can be an actual disadvantage if wrongly used.

One of its more effective uses in Malaya was in bringing government services and control to remote areas, as described in the last chapter. This task, though small, was significant. Other uses included the rapid movement of troops, the air supply of isolated garrisons and patrols, reconnaissance, psychological warfare, and offensive air strikes. The last, because of the terrain, was the least important of all in Malaya.

I have left the main discussion of air support until the rest of the story has been told, because air power is not an end in itself in counterinsurgency. It can contribute only by supporting other agencies—police, army, and civil government services.

Troop-carrying helicopters did not reach Malaya until 1953. Before then, our efforts in the remote areas were rather ineffective. When aborigines reported that guerrillas were based in a certain area, patrols on foot would take several days to get there. On arrival, they would find no enemy, but a friendly aborigine might say where they had gone. As the patrol moved on, another aborigine would get warning to the Communists, for which they would reward him generously. These aborigines knew the jungle well, and could skip quickly along the animal trails. Our patrols, even with guides, would fall far behind this enemy warning system.

The arrival of troop-carrying helicopters reversed this situation: the soldiers could reach the area long before the warning. Thereafter, the helicopters could move the patrols for reconnaissance of new areas, conduct their reliefs, and above all help them to win the support of the aborigines with medical attention and the beginnings of trade. I am convinced that we could never have cleared the guerrillas from the deep jungle without helicopters.

Second only to this in importance was the helicopters' ability to evacuate our own casualties, both from the teams in the jungle and from the routine patrols in the jungle fringe. A patch of secondary jungle could often be found which the patrol could clear with its own chain saws; but if not, a radio call for a few pounds of explosives would soon enable a clearance to be made even in a teak forest for a helicopter to get the wounded man out to a hospital. The knowledge that this could be done—instead of a ghastly journey on a stretcher—gave a tremendous boost to the morale of every soldier on patrol.

Similar methods were sometimes applied to getting quick intelligence from a captured guerrilla, either by flying him (or his documents) out, or by flying a Special Branch man in.

Reaction operations are another field in which helicopter transport can be decisive. In Malaya, this seldom applied to the main war around the villages, where the road system enabled wheeled transport to get troops there fast enough without attracting so much attention. Helicopters, however, made reaction operations in the jungle itself more efficient, though even here their value was as a *transport* rather than as a *tactical* device.

*Tactical* operations with helicopters, in fact, were seldom successful in Malaya because both in jungle and rubber the guerrillas could hear them coming early enough to get away or take up concealed ambush positions; but there is much more open ground in South Vietnam, and there was more still in Algeria, where the French used helicopters in the open mountain terrain with tremendous tactical success.[1]

The STOL[2] fixed-wing Scottish Aviation Pioneer aircraft we had in Malaya could carry 4 passengers or 800 pounds of cargo, was faster than a helicopter, took far less maintenance effort to back it, and had a cost effectiveness 10 times as good as a helicopter between places where it could take off and land.

The Pioneer could land on a 150-yard strip and climb steeply out of the sheer tree-covered valleys in which most deep jungle forts and posts were located. In remote areas, once the initial reconnaissances and patrols had made the aborigine pattern clear, army engineers could usually find patches of abandoned aborigine cultivation near the rivers where STOL strips could be cleared in a few weeks. Nearly all our jungle forts were thereafter maintained by Pioneer aircraft, which were also in extensive use for communication flights all over the country for army, police, and civilian officials, and for those Special Branch favorites, the surrendered enemy personnel.

---

[1] The French in Algeria had every troop-carrying helicopter fitted for rapid mounting of 20-mm. machine guns as an alternative to carrying troops. This gun enabled them to kill guerrillas from an altitude of 2,000 feet, where there was little risk from ground fire, and its quick mounting and removal gave them great flexibility in landing troops almost on top of formed guerrilla units. Tree cover was too close in Malaya for this to be effective except in the few large paddy-growing areas; and by the time we had our helicopters in any strength (1953), we already had the big enemy units under control with our ground troops. Such operations are now an important part of modern counterinsurgency, but their technique must be looked for from Vietnam and Algeria, rather than from Malaya.

[2] Short takeoff and landing. Another type used for less operational missions was the De Havilland Beaver, which was faster and more comfortable than the Pioneer, but needed a longer strip. This is the same as the U.S. Army's L-19.

Third only to helicopters and Pioneers in numbers of sorties[3] were the RAF Valetta transport aircraft, which in 1955 parachuted 4,000 tons of supplies into the jungle and airlifted 30,000 people with 250 tons of equipment. Losses of supplies for air drops were less than 2 per cent, though parachute costs were so high[4] that it was usually cheaper to make a STOL airstrip for static posts.

The casualty rate for crews on air-supply missions was higher than that of the infantry they supplied because of the steep valleys and frequent, sudden cloud formations. A fixed-wing aircraft entering the wrong valley was often doomed—it could neither climb out nor turn—and usually every man in it died. In spite of this, the crews took pride in ensuring that the troops never went hungry or without their mail and would allow neither weather nor terrain to deter them once their squadron had allowed them to take off. Searching for a tiny clearing, a smoke signal, or a colored balloon floating above the trees, they would have long radio chats with the patrols as they circled around; and great affection and respect grew up between these men, who knew each other's names but never met.

The SAS Regiment developed a method of parachuting into the treetops that had been originated by forest-fire fighters in North America. Each man carried a length of canvas webbing strap on which he could lower himself from the branches. His aim was to steer himself into the densest foliage rather than allow his parachute to be collapsed between two trees 200 feet in the air. In the drop of 60 men described in the Batu Bintang operation in Chapter 14, the only casualty was from this cause.

The advantage of this method was that troops could be introduced into the jungle without the guerrillas knowing they were there. (They almost always knew when helicopter landing zones were prepared.) The only precaution needed was a cover plan under which aircraft had used the route before for air-supply or communication flights.

---

[3] In the peak year (1955), numbers of sorties in Malaya were: helicopters, 20,000; Pioneers, 4,700; Valettas, 2,100.

[4] Parachutes were in theory recoverable but were made useless by even the smallest tear, those that hit the ground intact seldom survived the soldiers' pickup without a nick or two; they made superb mosquitoproof, lightweight sleeping bags.

RAF Valettas were also much used for psychological warfare. They dropped up to a million leaflets a day, seldom less than half a million. These were so effective in inducing surrenders that the Communists would shoot any guerrilla found in possession of one; so the voice aircraft, fitted with loudspeakers, were more effective still. The content of the leaflets and broadcasts was discussed in Chapter 12.

Helicopters, Pioneers, and the De Havilland Beavers were used for spraying weed-killer onto enemy cultivations. One limitation, however, was that sprayed (as opposed to injected) weed-killer works only through the leaves; the guerrillas were quick to pick off those affected, leaving the roots intact.[5]

Defoliation to deny the enemy cover was not done in Malaya by air spraying. The only areas where this could have been both practical and effective were the likely ambush sites along the roads; but that was more effectively done by hand, and there were always more urgent demands for aircraft.

Visual reconnaissance was done by Auster artillery observation aircraft, which were both maneuverable and reliable. Each pilot learned his way around a particular area and was sometimes able to spot signs of fresh trails, of wood cutting, or of water points on the streams. In the earlier days, the pilots sometimes saw smoke or even the ill-concealed roof of a *basha* (jungle shelter); but as the hunt became hotter, such indiscretions were rare.

The Austers were also used to help patrols fix their own positions. The patrols would raise a colored balloon or smoke signal; sometimes they carried radio beacons if an accurate fix was required.

Photoreconnaissance was chiefly useful in showing up new jungle cultivations or changes in the aborigine pattern. It also sometimes revealed fresh trails coming out of the jungle, particularly where the ground was open or swampy. Apart from this, it seldom gave much direct intelligence of guerrilla movements, though this would not be so in more open country than Malaya.

Except for occasional successes with pinpoint bombing, offensive air strikes were almost wholly unsuccessful in Malaya; they prob-

[5] M. C. A. Henniker, *Red Shadow over Malaya*, p. 180.

ably did more harm than good. Hundreds of tons of bombs were dropped on the jungle every month, particularly in 1951–52; they probably killed fewer than half a dozen guerrillas a year—more by accident than design. Such senseless swiping induced a feeling of contempt for the power of modern weapons, and the enemy made full use of this contempt in their propaganda among the villagers and aborigines who had heard all the noise.[6]

Worse still, if bombs were dropped in or near inhabited areas, the people's means of livelihood (rubber trees or cultivation) would be destroyed, and innocent people might be killed. One aborigine woman or child killed or maimed by bombing would leave a lasting scar on hundreds of "hearts and minds."

Inhabited villages were never shelled, strafed, or bombed in Malaya. It can be argued that such attacks are justified if troops entering the village are likely to be fired upon, or even as a punishment for harboring Communist guerrillas—whether or not such "harboring" was willing or coerced. It has even been argued that the people would, in fact, turn against the Communists for bringing it down on their heads. Fortunately, however, these arguments never prevailed in Malaya; if they had, I am quite sure that any villages so attacked would never have cooperated with the government again.

Villages have, however, frequently been shelled and bombed in South Vietnam.[7] Typical was a South Vietnamese Army report on operations in the Plain of Reeds and Zone D in 1963, in which they claimed 76 enemy killed by ground fire and 400 by aerial gunnery, but only 14 weapons captured and more than 400 houses and huts destroyed.[8] Bernard Fall suggests that part of the rationale for such attacks seems to be to show the people "that the Viet Cong could not live up to its promise to protect them"; he adds that many of the so-called Viet Cong who are killed may be innocent bystanders. He comments: "It apparently has been forgotten that these aircraft are not operating on foreign enemy targets, but upon a popu-

---

[6] The same applied to indiscriminate shelling of the jungle by artillery. Artillery was valuable in supporting the defense of forts, camps, posts, and patrol bases, but of little use in flushing mobile guerrilas out of dense jungle.

[7] I refer only to shelling and bombing of friendly territory—whether or not it is temporarily occupied by the enemy.

[8] *Times of Vietnam*, January 9, 1963.

lation whose allegiance Saigon must regain if it wishes to win this war."[9]

Much has changed since 1963. It is now clearly difficult to avoid situations in which Viet Cong units establish themselves in villages in regimental strength, and it becomes impossible to evict them without a major attack that includes artillery and air strikes. This is not guerrilla warfare but conventional war. Even so, the price that is paid for such attacks may be heavy in terms of popular support. A U.S. Army adviser writing from Vietnam in February, 1965, summed it up by saying: "Except against a pinpoint target such as VC troops in the open, air strikes and artillery are a question mark as to their value in counterinsurgency. We don't make any new friends by smashing a VC-occupied village."[10]

This ties in with our experience in Malaya, where the only successful bombing raids were those in which the target was clear of populated areas and so precisely fixed that a formation of bombers could drop a pattern of bombs tight enough to leave no gaps but still embracing the margin of error. There was so much cover that such targets never presented themselves to visual observation from the air; and when our troops or aircraft did make a fix accurate enough for this, they were without exception acting on information from an agent or surrendered guerrilla with personal knowledge of the enemy.

The first successful bombing raid of the war did not in fact occur until its eighth year—in February, 1956.[11] On an agent's information, an army patrol found an empty camp used by an independent MRLA platoon that was away on an operation. The patrol fixed it with great patience and accuracy, and the agent was told of the big rewards he might earn if he could tell them when the platoon had reoccupied the camp. He did. Five bombers flew straight over without circling and straddled the camp with 70 bombs of 1,000 pounds each. Of the 21 guerrillas in the camp, 14 were killed outright.

The following year, we developed a more accurate technique

---

[9] Fall, *The Two Viet-Nams,* p. 350.

[10] Lieutenant Don L. Lair, U.S. Army adviser in Quang Ngai Province, quoted in a letter from Major Osborn, February 18, 1965.

[11] This operation is described in vivid detail by the battalion commander who located the camp in Miers, *op. cit.,* chap. v.

for guiding the bombers onto the target by radar; then we were able to bomb by night, given an accurate fix on the map grid. This led to two more operations, each involving an agent. In one of them, a cool-headed patrol lay unobserved within 15 yards of an occupied camp while fixing its precise grid reference. The kill rate was even higher than in the daylight raids because the sleeping guerrillas did not move quickly enough when they heard the aircraft approaching. In one of them, nine of the ten in the camp were killed outright. In all three raids, the bombs killed an important enemy commander, the real target. This alone made the raids worthwhile because the best guerrilla leaders seemed always to get away in the ground ambushes.

In another case, a small radio beacon was planted skillfully near a guerrilla camp. The signals were picked up and fixed by triangulation from an Auster aircraft that was itself being tracked by ground radar stations. In spite of this somewhat cumbersome two-stage aerial fix, the accuracy proved to be within 100 yards, and so did the resultant pattern of bombs.

The bombers used were World War II, piston-engined Lincolns, which flew slowly but accurately, each carrying fourteen 1,000-pound bombs. Five Lincolns dropped a pattern of 70 bombs in a rectangle 400 yards wide by 1,000 yards long. They could be guided by radar with a probable error of less than 200 yards; given a precise fix on the ground, the theoretical chance of a hit was 100 per cent. So it proved, when all conditions were right—agent, fixation, surprise, and weather. Such a combination, however, was rare.

Later, the Lincolns were replaced by new jet bombers. These were too fast for the accuracy required, and there were no more successes like the ones described; but by that time, there were very few targets left.

It can be argued that if an insurgency reaches the stage where intelligence is good enough for this kind of operation, the enemy will by then have been so split up that worthwhile targets for precision bombing will never arise. If that argument were true, then there would be little point in having offensive strike aircraft in jungle terrain. This is an exaggeration. We certainly know enough about intelligence techniques now to build up an effective intelligence organization, even in the early days of an insurgency; and we can help any friendly government to do the same if it is prepared to give the necessary singlemindedness to the task. We also have the techniques to make pinpoint bombing effective. Unless we have either precise intelligence or good observation, however, offensive air strikes are a waste of time.

In open country, such as in Algeria or parts of Vietnam, air power can be decisive if used wisely, both as an offensive weapon and for transport. Used unwisely, however, it can do real harm, both in telegraphing our punches and in alienating the local population.

In Malaya, offensive air strikes and *tactical* air movement were never decisive. I do not believe they ever will be in a counterinsurgency in terrain that provides so much cover for guerrillas. Air supply did have a big influence on our war in the jungle fringe by enabling patrols to live there for weeks instead of days. But even this asset probably could have been obtained by using thousands of back-packing porters, as the Vietminh's General Giap did before Dien Bien Phu. It can be argued that we could have won the war around the villages without any air power at all.

Even if we had, however, the victory would not have been a lasting one. Air transport—more in its civil than in its purely military effects—was an indispensable part of our campaign in the deep jungle. But for this, the Communists would have been able to maintain their army intact to this day, based on the aborigine tribesmen, all down the mountain spine of Malaya. From there it could have emerged to terrorize the villagers at will, and the very existence of this threat would have been enough to keep the village Communist organizations alive. This would have been very serious indeed, because no government can maintain Emergency Regulations forever. This problem, small as it seemed in comparison with the war around the villages, was a vital one; and in this respect, air power in Malaya was one of the decisive factors.

# 19

## THE CRUMBLE AND
## THE HARD CORE

THE Duke of Edinburgh was being briefed in the operations room in Kuala Lumpur late in 1956. The war was quiet. There were not many more than 2,000 guerrillas still in the jungle, almost every one of whom was now recorded by name on police files. There were 20 battalions chasing them in the jungle, but on the average they were killing only one guerrilla a day.

"Yes, but how are you going to finish the thing off?"

The Duke got a rather lame answer, something about needles and haystacks. I am sure that no one in the room then had any idea how the thing was going to break, or just how complete our victory would be.

When guerrillas win, the pattern is clear enough: either there is a political settlement or the war blows up into a Dien Bien Phu. Even if a few loyalist diehards decide to continue guerrilla warfare in reverse, the people will seldom support this because they are sick of war and too scared of the new ex-guerrilla regime.

The big question in Malaya was whether the people (and the newly elected Malayan politicians) would put up with the Emergency Regulations long enough to break the Communist organization beyond hope of revival. In spite of Tunku Abdul Rahman's firm stand at the 1955 truce talks, many politicians were tired of the war and willing to take the risk of letting off the pressure. Communist sympathizers, of course, were hard at work behind the scenes to encourage them.

By 1956, most of the eastern half of the country was a white area, and tremendous efforts were being made to finish off the Communists in the center so that the nation's capital could be declared white by Merdeka Day. This was achieved; and when Tunku Abdul Rahman took over, the situation was as shown in Figure 6. The 2,000 guerrillas were mainly concentrated in three groups of 500, one astride the Thai border, the second in the northern state of Perak, and the third in the southern state of Johore. The remainder were spread out in small remnants of the Malayan Communist Party districts and branches in the jungle fringes over the rest of the black area.

The government's plan to finish off the weakest areas first had been launched in 1954, and the start of it was described in Chapter 13. Two years later, the main Communist organization astride the road through the tin and rubber area remained intact. Though the MRLA platoons had been reduced to a handful, the MCP branches and their supporters were still there. We had only to stop the treatment for the infection to spread all over again.

Down at the tip of South Johore, for example, one of our best battalion commanders had been thrashing the rubber and the jungle with 400 soldiers for six months, searching for a gang of five guerrillas led by an old woman Communist who dressed in rubber tapper's clothes and pulled her rifle along behind her on a string. When the tappers signaled the approach of soldiers, she would drop the string, whip out a tapping knife, and tap the nearest tree. She and her four companions ran a hierarchy of no less than 400 active supporters in her parish, and they had cowed the remainder of the villagers into keeping their mouths shut. The old woman was not eliminated until 1959.

With so many guerrillas still at large, the Merdeka celebrations were tinged with a note of anxiety for those concerned with finishing

### FIGURE 6
#### White Areas

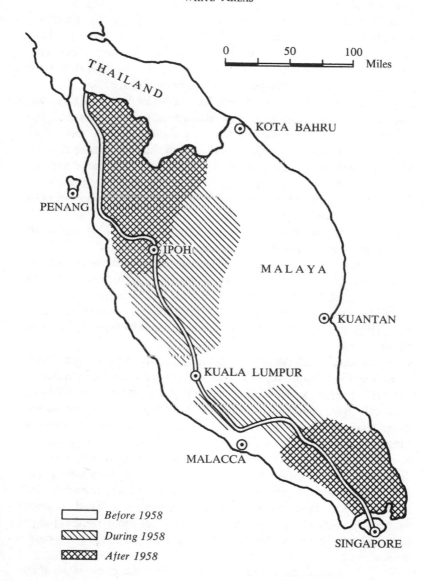

0       50      100
Miles

THAILAND

KOTA BAHRU

PENANG

IPOH

MALAYA

KUANTAN

KUALA LUMPUR

MALACCA

SINGAPORE

Before 1958
During 1958
After 1958

off the war; but the enemy had more problems than we thought. If we could only be patient and determined, something might break.

What broke was a pair of most unexpected members of the Communist hard core.

In October, 1957, six weeks after Merdeka Day, five guerrillas held up a British civilian on the road and asked him to drive them to the nearest police station. They seemed like any other surrendered enemy personnel, dirty and hungry, but in fact, they were the regional political commissar and his bodyguard.

The nearest police station was at a district headquarters that housed a brilliant young Special Branch officer. He resisted the temptation to boost local morale by announcing five more surrenders or to give the soldiers some quick kills, realizing that he had a prisoner who required special handling. With the details of the reward system dangling on the wall, he and the commissar worked out a plan that was to make the commissar one of the richest men in Malaya.

As regional political commissar, he had the task of visiting regularly every MCP branch and district committee in the whole of South Perak. His only means of doing this was to wait at their various jungle letter boxes on the days appointed for their couriers to call, then to be guided by each courier to the branch or district camp. So he alone, among all the guerrillas in the region, knew the site of every letter box and the day on which every courier called.

So, on the second Tuesday of the month, the political commissar, in his full Communist regalia, was waiting for a district courier at the first letter box. Concealed nearby was a patrol of soldiers, who duly followed the courier and the commissar to the camp. What went on inside will never be known. My guess is that he simply informed them that the Party had decided on a change of plan and the armed struggle was to be discontinued. For most of them, this, from a senior Party official, was enough; they were probably glad enough of the chance to come out. Whatever line he did in fact take in these tense jungle conferences, it worked. Branch by branch, district by district, every single element of the jungle hierarchy in the region trooped out of the jungle behind the commissar.

The whole procedure took six months. For the commissar, they were very exhausting months. The police knew that they must complete the process both before he was worn out and before the news of his surrender leaked out. After each operation, he would be given a break of a week or two, living in great security in a British police officer's house, chain-smoking to soothe his nerves, before setting out to meet the next courier and lead in the next branch. Probably the only thing that kept him going was the knowledge that the next ten guerrillas he brought in would add another 20,000 Malayan dollars to his fast-growing bank balance.

Apart from proving the value of the reward system, perhaps the biggest lesson of this story is its proof of the tightness of the Communist security system. So secret were the movements of the commissar that virtually no one knew anything about him until he appeared. Since the entire guerrilla unit then walked out with the commissar into police captivity, the news never spread. The fact that nothing more was heard from the branch committee in the coming months was not unusual; this usually just meant a dead courier or a mixup over letter boxes. Even the masses executives in the villages could assume that the branch was keeping away for good security reasons and getting what it needed from the other villages. Communists are taught to keep quiet and not to pry into things that do not concern them. The result was that the entire regional organization quietly slipped away without the MCP hierarchy knowing anything about it for six months.

A second "super SEP" came in just as these six months were finishing. He was an even more influential member of the hierarchy, this time in Johore. The method by which the police used him to bring in his command was roughly the same as for the regional commissar, but his motives were quite different. He made his own way to the police station, where he confidently outlined his plan. He had, he said, realized that the struggle was now useless; he wanted to end the slaughter of the men and women under his command. Reassured that the amnesty for SEP's really would be honored, he, too, embarked on a six-month program that brought in his entire command, unit by unit. Though no one can be certain of what goes on in a Communist's mind, I believe his motives were genuine; but he had no scruples about accepting the rewards, and he has used the capital to found a large and prosperous business in Singapore.

Between them, these two "super SEP's" were responsible for clearing almost the whole of the area marked on Figure 6 as "freed from emergency restrictions during 1958." Not a word was said while the operations were in progress. The figures of these surrenders were excluded from the continuing routine announcements of kills and surrenders elsewhere. To the public, the war appeared to have bogged down. It must have been galling for Tunku Abdul Rahman to endure the criticism that not much seemed to be happening in the first year of his independent rule, but he resisted the temptation to give even a hint of these spectacular developments. After a few months, the editors of the chief newspapers were told that something big was on and were asked not to speculate—and the press cooperated. When the story did break, it coincided with the declaration of a huge extension of the white areas.

The rest of the story of the crumble is quickly told. Overwhelming resources of soldiers and police could now be concentrated in the two small hard-core areas of North Perak and South Johore. Even the most loyal Communist supporters realized that the war was lost, and the bulk of the people in these two areas were ready to help the government get rid of the Emergency Regulations, which for everyone else in the country were now only a memory. By 1960, there were not more than twenty or thirty guerrillas still left in Malaya itself, and these were just pathetic beggars, living on the charity of the aborigines. The emergency was officially declared over, and all Emergency Regulations were lifted except those needed to guard against subversion.

What still remains are Chin Peng and his 400 guerrillas on the Thai border. Would any other army in the world have held out for so long? We all like to think that we would, but probably no body of men and women have shown such endurance since the early Christian martyrs. The Christians, however, had an absolute faith in life after death; the Communists have not even that.

What motivated that old woman who held out with four companions against 400 soldiers, plagued by defection and treachery among her supporters, knowing that she must inevitably die or be captured in the end? There were many others like her. Badly wounded Communists, who would squirm to avoid injections to relieve their pain, convinced that they were drugs to make them betray their cause, would die in agony spitting hatred and defiance in the faces of the doctors.

Our regional political commissar, the "super SEP," knew there was one district committee secretary who would never surrender (we will call him Ah Kong), so he arranged to lure him into an ambush. A hand-picked soldier was detailed to concentrate solely on Ah Kong, whose face and frame he knew well from photographs. He had him in the sights of his automatic rifle in broad daylight and knew that he had put five shots into his chest at point range, but Ah Kong ran away through the jungle. At dusk, the search was called off and the ambush party bedded down. During the night, they heard a single shot; next morning, they found that Ah Kong had killed himself rather than surrender. Besides the marksman's five in his chest, he carried eleven bullets from the others in the ambush plus his own.

In the pinpoint bombing raid described in Chapter 18,[1] the guerrilla platoon commander and all his section leaders were killed, with fourteen of the twenty-one men. Only a deputy section leader survived with six others. All were wounded; they had been in the middle of a tight pattern of bombs of the total power of a low-yield nuclear bomb. Nevertheless, the deputy section leader led them out with their weapons, eluded the ring of searching troops, survived an ambush in which he lost one man, and got the other five away into the deep jungle to recuperate with virtually no medical supplies. Despite their knowledge that comfortable hospital beds and an amnesty awaited them outside, not a man surrendered. Three months later, the same guerrilla led the men to the jungle fringe and launched his own recruiting campaign. Within a year, the platoon was back at full strength; it continued to operate under his leadership for the next two years. Such fortitude and leadership must be saluted, whatever its motive. The true Communist, the true believer, should never be underestimated or despised.

Chin Peng is such a man, and so no doubt are some of his diehards on the Thai border. Militarily, they are unlikely to be destroyed; nor, now, are they likely to surrender. Their religion reminds them that Lenin was in exile for sixteen years, Mao Tse-tung for eleven; that Communism must in the end encompass the world,

---

[1] See also Miers, *op. cit.,* chap. vi.

and it does not matter whether this is in their lifetime or not; that their duty is clear: to hold out so that they are ready to seize any chance to foster the cause if that chance does come before they die. If they die without it, they will die happy in the belief that they devoted their lives to the good of mankind.

Will the chance for these 400 ever come? They have a well-established base and accredited representatives in Indonesia through whom they have contact with the outside world. Should their aims coincide with those of the Indonesians, and if both of them consider that the time is ripe, they could undoubtedly march south and reappear on the jungle fringes around the Malayan Chinese villages. All will then depend upon whether they can re-build an efficient Communist underground organization in these villages.

It needs only half a dozen dedicated clandestine Communists to provide the nucleus—the masses executives—for a village organization. These half dozen will undoubtedly exist in almost every Malayan Chinese village, just as they do in other communities all over the world. For the time being, they are probably doing little more than keeping contact with each other, and doing some quiet work in front organizations; they will also be maintaining lists of potential supporters and targets for blackmail and subversion. They are well experienced in leadership, exploitation, and coercion, and they could quickly recruit a substantial masses organization if Chin Peng were to need it.

Nevertheless, I believe that such an organization would be hard put to survive—anyway for some years to come—because the Chinese villagers remember the price that they and their families had to pay for guerrilla warfare in the 1950's, and most of them will not want to see it start again. Should the guerrillas reappear across the jungle fringe, I believe that there will be no shortage of rubber tappers ready to report them, provided that the government continues to maintain an adequate police force to protect them and an efficient Special Branch to obtain and use their information.

Subversion—in the towns as well as in the villages—remains the more serious danger, and the Federation Government is fully alive to this. So long as the safety valve of political freedom continues to exist, however, I believe that this, too, can be kept under control by the Special Branch.

Chin Peng's real hope must lie in exploiting internal racial conflict or outside interference. Lenin was given his chance by the Germans, and Mao Tse-tung by the Japanese. A dramatic turn of events could bring Communist government to the borders where Chin Peng is waiting, or to Indonesia, which is only twelve miles across the Straits from Singapore. And he will be taking particular interest in Singapore. His hopes of its subversion, high in 1962, dashed by its merger with Malaya in 1963, must have been revived by the break-up of that merger in 1965, and by the racial and political rivalries revealed by the break. Chin Peng has taken a beating but he is not dead.

# 20

## CONCLUSIONS

THE Mao Tse-tung plan follows a clear pattern. Is there a pattern for beating it? Though varying conditions and methods mean that any pattern must be applied with great care, we discern a line of action that can counter each phase of the Mao Tse-tung plan; we also see the likely effect if that action succeeds. (See Figure 7.)

Communist subversion to build up a popular base for insurgency is going on in many places. Where there is good government and a good intelligence system, it makes little progress, there is no insurgency. Where these things do not exist, the government may not even know the process is going on until trouble breaks out in the form of rioting or in the disruption of local administration by murder and intimidation, such as developed in South Vietnam after 1956.

If out of this situation the Communists can seize power by a

# FIGURE 7
## A PATTERN OF COUNTERINSURGENCY

| COMMUNIST PLAN | GOVERNMENT COUNTERMEASURES | | EFFECT ON COMMUNISTS |
|---|---|---|---|
| Organize underground support among the people, with parallel hierarchy to control them | Good local government and intelligence system | | Prevents establishment of popular base |
| Rioting, sabotage, intimidation. *coup d'état* if possible | Emergency regulations, including registration of population and powers of detention | | Prevents *coup d'état*, forces leaders and armed Communists out of towns and villages |
| If coup fails, take to jungle or mountains | Protect and control population, harass big guerrilla units to make them split up | | Guerrilla warfare on a falling scale |
| | Thereafter: | | |
| | *If Losing Ground* | *If Winning Ground* | |
| Guerrilla warfare on rising scale | Try to retain police posts and local government in every village. Take advantage of guerrillas' concentrating into big units to find and destroy them. If government control is lost in a large area, re-establish it village by village, dealing with the easiest first. Then resume winning cycle | Develop intelligence system | Revert to terror and subversion to keep hold on people until government loses determination |
| Form "liberated" areas | | Concentrate pressure to clear easiest areas first | Growing flow of intelligence and increasing guerrilla surrenders |
| Build up conventional forces | | Patient determination and progressive government; lift restrictions as each area is cleared | Collapse of public support, area by area |
| Defeat government forces | | | |

*coup d'état,* they will. This can be prevented by prompt and firm emergency legislation (see Chapter 5), backed by a police and administrative system able to enforce it.

When this happens, as in Malaya, the Communists will switch to guerrilla warfare—Mao Tse-tung's "protracted war." Thereafter, if government countermeasures are inadequate, the guerrillas will gain control of "liberated areas" and be converted into conventional units that can knock out the government forces, as in North Vietnam in 1954.

The first reaction to guerrilla warfare must be to protect and control the population. An extension of the emergency legislation will usually include some form of resettlement. The key is the survival of village police posts, from which the streets can be effectively patrolled by night. Their survival must be supported by military action aimed at forcing the guerrilla units to split up.

If these measures gain ground, the scale of guerrilla warfare will subside and aggressive raids on villages will give place to clandestine terror and subversion. To defeat this and root out the small guerrilla units takes a long time, during which many unpopular emergency regulations must be kept in force. If the government gives in too soon to public and political pressure to relax these regulations, the Communist organization will revive and resume its growth. On the other hand, patient determination, progressive government, and a good intelligence system can eventually destroy it, as was proved in Malaya. The key in this phase is the police intelligence branch.

Should these measures fail, the guerrilla units will become bigger and more aggressive, but at the same time more vulnerable to conventional attack from ground and air. These big units must be destroyed without irrevocably alienating the population. There must, above all, be absolute determination to establish and retain a government police post intact and uncorrupt in every inhabited village. Should it be destroyed, it must be replaced. If whole areas become untenable, then the rest of the country must be held; authority must be re-established patiently, village by village, into the "liberated" area, dealing with the easiest areas first. It takes time, but it can be done if the people can be convinced by practical means that it is in their interest for the government to win.

This is the pattern. Every revolutionary movement, whether Communist or not, borrows the Communists' professional techniques. The same pattern has been discernible through the fog of almost every insurgency since 1949.[1] The same thread can be followed in Malaya, Vietnam, the Philippines, Kenya, Cyprus, and Algeria.

People directing a counterinsurgency are often in need of indicators of progress—or danger signs—to guide their actions. I believe that the insurgencies in North Vietnam, Malaya, and South Vietnam have produced four such reliable indicators of progress against the Mao Tse-tung plan.

The first is the degree to which the local government is able to do an honest job and enforce the rule of law. It is quite easy to detect when reassuring reports are false. Where the local government and police can survive only by turning a blind eye to the enemy, that village is a Communist village.

Second is the size in which guerrilla units live and operate. In North Vietnam they grew, declined, and grew again—up to divisional strength. In Malaya, they declined—to platoon strength. In South Vietnam, they have grown from year to year. Though air power may keep them from growing above battalion or regimental strength, both of these are much too big for village defenses to hold off. It is at company strength (100) that they become dangerous, and so long as they can live in company groups, they will tend to grow bigger all the time, until massive conventional operations are needed to deal with them.

Third is the flow of information from the people. This is both an indicator of confidence and a battle-winning factor.

So, too, is the fourth—the rate of surrender of *genuine* guerrillas. This can be a misleading indicator if the temporary compliance of previously hostile villagers is credited as surrender. As a battle-

---

[1] The revolutions in Eastern Europe and elsewhere before 1949 followed the earlier stages—the Russian model—though some were already responding to the influence of Mao Tse-tung's writings. Even the numerous Latin American revolutions are based on the Russian model, though many of these are no more than mock fights, staged by mutual agreement to give the outgoing dictator a plausible excuse to bail out quickly with his profits before unpopularity takes them from him, and to give his successor an excuse to establish himself with martial law so that he can start building up his own.

winning factor, it can quickly be thrown away if the surrendered guerrillas are not handled well.

So far all these indicators—excepting sometimes the fourth—have pointed depressingly in the wrong direction throughout both the wars in Vietnam—against the Vietminh and against the Viet Cong—so both wars have escalated. The escalation in North Vietnam succeeded, so a different answer is being tried to the escalation in South Vietnam. Meanwhile, the infighting continues, to destroy the guerrillas, to eliminate the parallel hierarchy, and to establish viable local government. Nothing will remove the necessity for completing these tasks, which will take years.

The decisive element in doing all these things in Malaya was the police force; counterinsurgency is a matter of restoring law and order, and law and order is a matter for policemen with the training and the lawful status for the task—not for part-time armed villagers. Security and intelligence were provided by the police, for whom the army was a support but not a substitute. There has been no real equivalent to the Malayan police force in South Vietnam; something like it must eventually be formed if the government is to win the war and keep the peace.

The way in which the war is won decides how long the peace will last. Ultimately, it is the people who decide; and shortcuts may do more harm than good. The quickest way to get immediate information from a captured guerrilla or from an arrested supporter is by torture, but this is a fatal mistake in the long run. The quickest way to stop a village supplying the guerrillas is to shoot ten hostages, take ten more, and tell the people that this will continue until they stop. They will stop, but they will hate the government that did this to them—not only for a few years but for a whole generation. The village will be ready to welcome anyone who will rid them of that government in the future.

Chin Peng in Malaya, like Mao Tse-tung in China, will assuredly try to come back. Had we been more ruthless in our methods, the government we helped to establish would have inherited the blame. The people would then have welcomed the returning Chin Peng as a savior; in the end, we would have made quite sure of losing the war.

We chose the other way. It took us a long time to win, but I believe that Malaya is now inoculated against Communism for many years to come. If Chin Peng comes back and pokes his nose out of the jungle fringe, a prosperous people will tell him to go away— and then they will inform the police. That is the real measure of a victory over insurgency.

# APPENDIXES

# APPENDIX A

# CHRONOLOGICAL SUMMARY
# OF EVENTS

## FIRST PERIOD: 1928-45

### FORMATION AND DEVELOPMENT OF THE
### MALAYAN COMMUNIST PARTY (MCP)

*1928*   South Seas Communist Party established in Singapore.

*1930*   South Seas Party renamed Malayan Communist Party (MCP) directed by Far Eastern Bureau of Russian Communist Party in Shanghai. Ho Chi Minh attends Party conference in Singapore.

*1931*   Intelligence coup in Singapore leads to widespread arrests of Communists in Singapore, Hong Kong, and Shanghai, including Ho Chi Minh (who was imprisoned in Hong Kong).

*1934*   Lai Tek joins MCP in Singapore.

*1939*   Lai Tek becomes Secretary General of MCP.

*1941*

*June*   Russia joins Western alliance on invasion by Germany.
         MCP (Lai Tek) offers to cooperate with British in Singapore.

*Dec.*   Japanese invasion of Malaya.
         200 Communists trained by British as stay-behind guerrillas (later named Malayan People's Anti-Japanese Army).

*1942*
*Feb.*    Fall of Singapore.
*Aug.*    Majority of MCP Central Committee arrested by Japanese in
          Singapore.
*Sept.*   90 leading Malayan Communists massacred by Japanese in
          Batu caves.
*1943*    British Force 136 (Colonel John Davis) joins MPAJA to train
          guerrillas and organize supply of weapons, ammunition, etc.,
          by parachute and submarine. Chin Peng acts as MPAJA liai-
          son officer.
*1945*
*Aug.*    Japanese surrender forestalls British landings. MPAJA seizes
          control from Japanese in some areas.
*Sept.*   British military government re-establishes control.
*Dec.*    MPAJA disbands. Guerrillas rewarded on handing in weapons,
          but retain large hidden dumps of other weapons and supplies
          in the jungle.
          MPAJA "Old Comrades' Association" maintains shadow guer-
          rilla army.

### SECOND PERIOD: 1946–60

| THE WAR AGAINST COMMUNISM | POLITICAL DEVELOPMENTS |
|---|---|
| *1946* | *1946* |
| Rival Kuomintang and Communist bandit gangs extorting money. Communist subversion through front organizations, schools, and trade unions. | British Government imposes Malayan Union, lowering status of Malay Sultans and offering full citizenship to immigrant races (Chinese and Indians), with declared aim of self-government. Malays boycott inauguration of Union and Dato Onn bin Jaafar forms United Malay National Organization (UMNO) to oppose it. |
| *1947* | |
| *March* Lai Tek disappears. Chin Peng becomes Secretary | |

General of MCP. 300 major strikes in year.

**1948**

**March** Communist conference in Calcutta decides on armed revolution throughout Southeast Asia. Outbreaks of rioting, sabotage, and assassination in Malaya.

**May** Legislation to curb Communist control of trade unions.

**June** MCP orders mobilization. Ex-members of MPAJA recalled to reform 8 regiments of guerrilla army with Minh Yuen (people's organization) to support them.

Government declares state of emergency. Emergency Regulations include 100 per cent registration of adult population and power to detain without trial.

**1949**

**Jan.** Output of new trainees raises police strength from 9,000 to 50,000.

Extra army units from Britain.

**April** Chin Peng's hope of a popular rising fails.

Communist army withdraws into deep jungle to regroup. Renamed "Malayan Races' Liberation Army" (MRLA).

Sharp fall in terrorist activity gives rise to premature optimism.

**1948**

**Feb.** British Government abandons plan for Malayan Union.

Federation of Malaya formed, consisting of the 9 Malay states and 2 British settlements of Penang and Malacca. (Singapore remains separate colony, as its predominantly Chinese population would swamp Malay majority in Federation.)

Malayan members join Executive and Legislative councils, and are given increasing responsibility for administration.

**1949**

**Feb.** Malayan Chinese Association (MCA) formed by Tan Cheng Lok. Aims to attract village Chinese away from Communism, in view of collapse of Kuomintang.

Chinese commercial community raises $2.5 million by lottery for MCA to improve conditions in Chinese villages.

*Oct.*  MRLA resumes offensive, operating in big units to terrorize population into acquiescence and to oust police from villages. British-Malayan Army, also operating in big units, fails either to kill guerrillas or to prevent terrorism.

*1950*

Terrorist murders of civilians rise to 100 per month.

*April*  General Sir Harold Briggs appointed Director of Operations, to control all counterinsurgency operations—civil, police, and military. Resettlement of 423,000 isolated Chinese squatters into New Villages begins.

*1951*

*Oct.*  Violence reaches peak with assassination of High Commissioner. Meanwhile, army units operating in smaller patrols forcing big guerrilla units to split up. MCP issues directive switching emphasis from wholesale violence to selective terror and subversion.

*Nov.*  Resettlement completed. Sir Harold Briggs retires and dies soon afterward.

*1952*

*Feb.*  General Sir Gerald Templer appointed as combined High Commissioner and Director of Operations. British reiterate that

*1951*

Dato Onn abandons UMNO and forms multiracial Independence of Malaya Party (IMP). Tunku Abdul Rahman becomes President of UMNO.

*1952*

*Feb.*  Elections for city and village councils, which become wholly Malayan. UMNO and MCA form electoral Alliance and win independence is aim for Malaya.

Incident rate begins to fall as Briggs Plan takes effect. Many more guerrillas being killed as a result of information from the people and from surrendered guerrillas.

9 of 11 seats on Kuala Lumpur Municipal Council. IMP wins only 2.

Malayan Indian Congress (MIC) joins Alliance, combining all three Malayan races in one party.

*1953*

Communist losses reach a peak with growing number of police agents among supporters.

First jungle forts established in aborigine areas, with arrival of helicopter squadrons.

First white area declared —freed from Emergency Regulations.

*1953*

Alliance Party demands self-government at once, independence within 3 years. It demands that during self-government period 60 per cent of members of Legislative Council should be elected, leaving 40 per cent nominated by High Commissioner until independence.

*1954*
*June*

Templer returns to Britain having wiped out two-thirds of guerrilla strength. Incident rate and murder rate cut to 20 per cent of 1951 peak.

*1954*

Templer announces that first elections for self-government will be in 1955, with 52 elected and 46 nominated members.

*1955*

Plan launched to clear weakest areas first, leaving hard core till last.

*June*    Chin Peng makes indirect overtures for peace talks.

*July*    Tunku Abdul Rahman becomes Chairman of Emergency Operations Council, taking over direction of war.

*Dec.*    Truce talks. Tunku Abdul Rahman refuses to

*1955*
*March*   Singapore becomes self-governing with elected majority in legislature, still separate from Federation.

*July*    Alliance Party wins 51 of 52 elected seats in Legislative Council and takes majority control of Executive Council, with Tunku Abdul Rahman as Chief Minister.

agree to Communists' operating as a legal political party, talks break down.

High Commissioner retains power of veto until full independence (1957) but never uses it.

*1956*

Most of eastern Malaya is declared white area. Troops withdrawn to concentrate on blacker areas in turn.

*1956*

Date for independence and draft constitution agreed on in London.

*1957*

White area extended across the center of the country, including Kuala Lumpur.

*1957*

*Aug. 31* Merdeka (Independence) Day. High Commissioner leaves. Tunku Abdul Rahman becomes Prime Minister.

*1958*

Crumble begins with collapse of all but hard-core areas, largely due to exploitation of two high-ranking surrendered Communists.

*1959*

All troops concentrated on two hard-core areas.

*1959*

At first postindependence elections in Malaya, Alliance Party wins 74 of 104 seats.
Lee Kuan Yew's People's Action Party (PAP) wins Singapore election with increased powers of self-government, calls for merger with Federation.

*1960*

State of emergency ends, with all Malaya cleared of guerrillas except for Chin Peng and 400 survivors astride Thai border.

## THIRD PERIOD: 1961–65

*1961*

*May*   Tunku Abdul Rahman proposes formation of Malaysia.

*Nov.*   Tunku Abdul Rahman and Lee Kuan Yew exchange heads of agreement for merger between Malaya and Singapore.

Dr. Subandrio, Indonesian Foreign Minister, informs United Nations that his government has no objection to inclusion of British North Borneo dependencies in Malaysia.

Government of Philippines claims part of North Borneo.

*1962*

Britain finds majority of North Borneo peoples want merger with Malaya and agrees to proposal.

*Sept.*   Singapore referendum shows 71 per cent favor merger.

*Dec.*   Revolt in Brunei fails. Indonesia declares "confrontation" policy.

*1963*

*April*   Indonesian guerrillas start raiding North Borneo territories (Sabah and Sarawak).

*July*   Manila accord. President Sukarno of Indonesia pledges support for Malaysia if U.N. Secretary General ascertains that it has popular support in Sabah and Sarawak.

*Aug.*   U.N. mission arrives in Sabah and Sarawak.

*Sept.*   U.N. Secretary General announces popular majority supports Malaysia. Malaysia inaugurated, with Singapore, Sabah, and Sarawak becoming independent from Britain and joining enlarged Federation.

Sukarno withdraws diplomatic status from Federation's ambassador in Indonesia.

Lee Kuan Yew re-elected with 37-to-14 majority.

*1964*

*April*   Tunku Abdul Rahman re-elected with increased majority (89 to 15).

Indonesian guerrillas land on mainland of Malaya, get no popular support, and are quickly mopped up.

*1965*

*Jan.*   Government of Philippines agrees to recognize Malaysia if Malaysia will submit their dispute over Sabah to the International Court.

Indonesia withdraws from U.N. on election of Malaysia to Security Council, concentrates troops as if for an invasion of Malaysia.

*Aug.*      Malaysian Government asks Singapore to leave the Federation, and Lee Kuan Yew agrees to do so. Singapore becomes an independent state, but Lee Kuan Yew promises close economic and defense cooperation with Malaysia, and asks that the British base remain.

# APPENDIX B

# ABBREVIATIONS

| | |
|---|---|
| DWEC | District War Executive Committee |
| EOC | Emergency Operations Council |
| IMP | Independence of Malaya Party |
| MCA | Malayan Chinese Association |
| MCP | Malayan Communist Party |
| MIC | Malayan Indian Congress |
| MIO | Military Intelligence Officer |
| MPAJA | Malayan People's Anti-Japanese Army |
| MRLA | Malayan Races' Liberation Army |
| PAP | People's Action Party |
| PMIP | Pan-Malayan Islamic Party |
| SEP | Surrendered Enemy Personnel |
| SWEC | State War Executive Committee |
| UMNO | United Malay National Organization |
| VC | Viet Cong |

# BIBLIOGRAPHY

# BIBLIOGRAPHY

## I. MALAYA—POLITICAL AND SOCIAL

HAN SUYIN. *And the Rain My Drink.* London: Jonathan Cape; New York: Little, Brown and New American Library, 1956. 319 pp.

The author is a woman doctor of mixed French-Chinese extraction, who worked in a Chinese village in one of the blackest areas in Malaya. Her book, written as a novel, gives a vivid picture of a rubber tapper's life in Malaya in 1952, pounded between two giants, the police and the Communists. She dislikes both giants, and she has a particularly bitter hatred for the informers and surrendered guerrillas who betray their comrades. This book captures the atmosphere of guerrilla warfare in and around the villages better than any I know.

KENNEDY, J. *A History of Malaya.* London: Macmillan; New York: St Martin's Press, 1962. 311 pp.

Only the final chapter (27 pages) is devoted to the period of the emergency (1946–59), but the book is recommended to those who want to study the history of Malaya.

MILLER, HARRY. *The Communist Menace in Malaya.* London: George Harrap; New York: Frederick A. Praeger, 1954. 238 pp.

A comprehensive account of the background, the outbreak, and the crisis of the Malayan insurgency (up to 1954) by a newspaperman who lived in Malaya throughout the period. The best book of its kind.

MILLS, LENNOX A. *Malaya—A Political and Economic Appraisal.* Minneapolis: The University of Minnesota Press, 1958. 234 pp.

This book gives an excellent account of the emergence of Malaya to independence with a stable government and a sound economy. It is particularly valuable to those who wish to study how the problems of racial, religious, and political rivalries were resolved and how a strong leader came to the top and earned overwhelming popular support.

PYE, LUCIAN W. *Guerrilla Communism in Malaya.* Princeton, N.J.: Princeton University Press, 1956. 363 pp.

The author, an American professor of political science, interviewed sixty surrendered guerrillas in Malaya and made this masterly analysis of their reasons for joining, their disillusionment, and their subsequent decisions to surrender. Throws a revealing light on Communist methods of subversion and on the psychology of Chinese guerrilla fighters.

SINGH, KERNIAL. "The Saga of the Malayan Squatter," *Journal of South East Asian History* (Singapore University), V, No. 1 (March, 1964), 143–77.

An analysis of the organization and execution of resettlement in Malaya, and of its social effects.

## II. MALAYA—POLICE AND MILITARY

CRAWFORD, OLIVER. *The Door Marked Malaya.* London: Rupert Hart-Davis, 1958. 237 pp.

A platoon commander's story by a young Oxford history graduate who did his national service with an infantry battalion in Malaya in 1954–55. All the other military books on this list are by mature professional soldiers. This one reveals the impact of guerrilla warfare on a sensitive young civilian with the sharp brain and natural bravery that are the qualities of the best counterinsurgent soldier. The atmosphere of the tiny battles in the jungle is evocatively described by one who understood their significance.

HENNIKER, M. C. A. *Red Shadow over Malaya.* Edinburgh: William Blackwood, 1955. 303 pp.

A brigade commander's account of operations by British and Gurkha troops in the days of Templer's triumph (1952–54), when the back of the guerrilla army was being broken. Particularly good in showing the workings of civil-police-military cooperation in the War Executive Committees.

MIERS, RICHARD. *Shoot to Kill.* London: Faber and Faber, 1959; New York: London House & Maxwell, 1962. 215 pp.

Richard Miers commanded a highly successful battalion in the final stages (1956–58) of hunting out the guerrillas and their supporters in the villages. Excellent on population control, village intelligence, and patrol tactics; contains an account of a successful pinpoint-bombing attack.

MORAN, J. W. G. *Spearhead in Malaya.* London: Peter Davies, 1959. 288 pp.

A police lieutenant's story, written about the operations of a jungle squad in the bad days of 1951 before the Briggs Plan had begun to have its effect. It reveals the problems of a British officer commanding Asian policemen and his frustrations in working with no intelligence other than what he creates for himself.

OLDFIELD, J. B. *The Green Howards in Malaya 1949–52.* Aldershot, England: Gale and Polden, 1953. 191 pp.

A factual account, in diary form, of every successful operation, kill by kill, by an infantry battalion in the second, third, and fourth years of the emergency. It shows how their tactics developed from their first fruitless flounderings in 1949; how they began to operate in smaller numbers, using greater stealth and skill; and how different things became when this was combined with the first trickles of information from the people.

## III. RELATED SUBJECTS

*Aggression from the North.* ("Publications of the United States Department of State," No. 7839.) Washington, D.C., 1964. 31 pp.

Thirty-six questions and answers about U.S. policy in Vietnam. Released August, 1964.

CONDIT, D. M. *et al.* (eds.). *A Counterinsurgency Bibliography.* Washington, D.C.: Special Operations Research Office, The American University, 1961.

The best bibliography I know on counterinsurgency up to 1961, this includes a few lines describing the content of each article and book listed.

FALL, BERNARD B. *Street Without Joy: Insurgency in Indochina 1946–1963*. 3d rev. ed. Harrisburg, Pa.: Stackpole; London: Pall Mall Press, 1964. 322 pp.

The French defeat in Indochina, describing particularly the later stages showing the escalation from guerrilla fighting to conventional warfare at Dien Bien Phu. How not to fight an insurgency, politically and militarily.

————. *The Two Viet-Nams: A Political and Military Analysis*. Rev. ed. New York: Frederick A. Praeger; London: Pall Mall Press, 1964. 493 pp.

A full political and military analysis of the development of the conflict between North and South Vietnam and of U.S. participation. Includes historical background, a wealth of reference material, and some penetrating comments.

GUEVARA, CHE. *Guerrilla Warfare*. Introduction by MAJOR HARRIES-CLICHY PETERSON, USMCR. New York: Frederick A. Praeger, 1961; London: Cassell (published as a joint volume with MAO TSE-TUNG, *Guerrilla Warfare*), 1962. 120 pp.

The Cuban interpretation of the protracted war. Che Guevara describes how a revolutionary situation can be created. He considers the rural pattern of insurgency the most effective for Latin America, as it has been for Asia.

LAWSON, RICHARD. *Strange Soldiering*. London: Hodder and Stoughton, 1963. 176 pp.

About the Congo. An awful warning of what can happen if political independence comes too soon, in particular, of how great a crime this is against the ordinary people who suffer in the resulting chaos. Written by a young British officer serving with the U.N.

MAO TSE-TUNG. *Guerrilla Warfare*. Translated by S. B. GRIFFITHS. New York: Frederick A. Praeger, 1961; London: Cassell (published as a joint volume with CHE GUEVARA, *Guerrilla Warfare*), 1962. 114 pp.

Extracts from the "bible" of Chinese-style guerrilla warfare written by Mao Tse-tung during his fight against the Japanese invaders.

OSANKA, FRANKLIN MARK (ed.). *Modern Guerrilla Warfare: Fighting Communist Guerrilla Movements, 1941–1961*. New York: The Free Press of Glencoe, 1962. 519 pp.

A comprehensive anthology of thirty-seven articles and extracts from books covering guerrilla warfare all over the world from 1941 to 1961. Includes a full bibliography on each insurgency, including Malaya.

OSBORNE, MILTON E. *Strategic Hamlets in South Viet-Nam—A Survey and a Comparison*. Ithaca, N.Y.: Cornell University Press, April, 1965. 66 pp.

A comparison of resettlement in Malaya and Vietnam.

TANHAM, GEORGE K. *Communist Revolutionary Warfare: The Vietminh in Indochina*. New York: Frederick A. Praeger, 1961. 176 pp.

The Vietminh interpretation of Mao Tse-tung's theory of protracted war and its triumphant execution in Indochina, 1946–54. Includes full accounts of the organization and recruitment of the Vietminh political and military machines.

*Vietnam—The Struggle for Freedom*. ("Publications of the United States Department of State," No. 7724.) Washington, D.C., 1964. 31 pp.

Thirty-six questions and answers about U.S. policy in Vietnam. Released August, 1964.

# INDEX

# INDEX